Journeys
of Love

Journeys of Love

30 TRUE STORIES
of Undeniable Devotion

Collected by Allison Gappa Bottke
Founder of the God Allows U-Turns Project,
with Cheryll Hutchings

BARBOUR
PUBLISHING

Our mission is to publish and distribute inspirational products offering exceptional value and biblical encouragement to the masses.

Member of the
Evangelical Christian
Publishers Association

Contents

Introduction

Sometimes it is difficult to see God when our lives are a mess. I did not see God when my first husband was dragging me up a flight of stairs by my hair, leaving bald and bloody patches on my scalp; or when I ached from punches and kicks; or when my husband held a knife to my throat or a gun to my head. I had no doubt—if God existed, He certainly did not exist in my world.

After the birth of my son and my divorce, both happening when I was sixteen, I tried to fill my soul with empty promises and pursuits. By the time I reached my late twenties, another marriage and divorce, several broken engagements, and more than one abortion had left me suicidal.

I was, as the song says, "looking for love in all the wrong places." But in the summer of 1989, I finally looked in the right place: I walked into a Wednesday evening church service.

I began to cry when I looked toward the pulpit and saw the statue of Jesus with outstretched hands, looking right at me. The pastor said we did not have to be lost, without direction, hope, and faith. He said we needed only to ask Jesus Christ to come into our hearts and He would be there—just like that.

That day I found God's redemption and freedom. He forgave the sins that weighed on my heart and filled the empty place in my life with His love. I learned it is never too late to change direction, because God loves us and allows U-turns!

The stories you are about to read are as varied as the people who have written them. We pray that within these pages you will find a confirmation of God's love for you and a reminder of how He sometimes shows His love through others in your life.

ALLISON GAPPA BOTTKE

In God's Eyes
by Candace Carteen, Portland, Oregon

My dad was ugly, and I knew it. By the time I was ten, I was totally ashamed of my father. My friends called him names: Quasimodo, hunchback, monster, little Frankenstein, the crooked little man. At first it hurt when they called him those things, but soon I agreed with them.

My father was born with parastremmatic dwarfism. The disease made him stop growing when he was about thirteen and caused his body to twist into a grotesque shape. When he was my age, pictures show him as a little short but good-looking. When he married my mother at nineteen, he still looked normal. He walked with a slight limp but could do just about anything. He was even a great dancer.

Soon after my birth, another genetic disorder took over, and his left foot started turning out, almost backward. His head and neck shifted to the right; his neck became rigid and he looked over his left shoulder a bit. His right arm curled in and up, and his index finger almost touched his elbow. His spine warped to look something like a roller coaster, causing his torso to lie sideways instead of straight up and down like that of a normal person. His walk became slow, awkward, and deliberate. He almost had to drag his left foot as he used his deformed right arm to balance his gait.

I hated to be seen with him. Everyone stared and seemed to pity me. I felt he must have done something really bad to have God hate him enough to deform his body.

By the time I was seventeen, I blamed all of my problems on my father. I didn't have the right boyfriends because of him. I didn't drive the right car because of him. I wasn't pretty enough because of him. I didn't have the right jobs because of him. I wasn't happy because of him. I knew if my father had been good-looking like Jane's father, or successful like Paul's father, or worldly like Terry's father, I would be perfect!

The night of my senior prom, Father had to place one more nail in my coffin—he had volunteered to chaperone at the dance. My heart sank when he told me. I stormed to my room, slammed the door, threw myself on the bed, and cried.

"Three more weeks and I'll be out of here!" I screamed into my pillow. "Three more weeks and I'll be at college! God, please make my father go away and leave me alone. Just make him disappear so I can have a good time at the dance."

I got dressed, my date picked me up, and we went to the prom. Father followed in his car. When we arrived, Father vanished into the pink chiffon drapes hanging in the auditorium. I thanked God that He had heard my prayer.

At least now I could have some fun.

Midway through the dance, Father came out from behind the drapes and started dancing with my friends. One by one, he took their hands and led them to the dance floor. He clumsily moved them in circles as the band played. Now *I* tried to vanish into the drapes.

After my friend Jane danced with him, she headed my way.

Oh no! I thought. *She's going to tell me he stomped on her foot or something.*

"Grace," she called, "you have the greatest father."

She smiled at me and grabbed my shoulders. "Your father's just the best. He's funny, kind, and always finds the time to be where you need him. I wish my father was more like that."

For one of the first times in my life, I couldn't talk. "What do you mean?" I asked her.

Jane looked at me strangely. "What do *you* mean? Your father's wonderful. I remember when we were kids and I'd sleep over at your house. He'd always come into your room and read us a book. I'm not sure my father can even read." She sighed and smiled. "Thanks for sharing him."

Then Jane ran off to dance with her boyfriend. I stood there in silence.

A few minutes later, my friend Paul joined me. "He's sure having a lot of fun," he said.

"Who is having a lot of fun?" I asked.

"Your father. He's having a ball."

"Yeah. I guess." I didn't know what else to say.

"You know, he's always been there," Paul said. "I remember when you and I were on the soccer team. He tried out as the coach, but he couldn't run up and down the field, remember? So they picked Jackie's father. But your dad still showed up for every game. He was the team's biggest fan. I think he's the reason we won so many games. Without him, it just would have been Jackie's father yelling at us. Your father made it fun. I wish my father had come to at least one of our games. He was always too busy."

I was once again speechless.

My boyfriend came back with two glasses of punch and handed me one.

"What do you think of my father?" I asked out of the blue.

Terry looked surprised. "I like him. I always have."

"Then why did you call him names when we were kids?"

"I don't know. Because he was different, and I was a dumb kid."

"When did you stop calling him names?" I asked, searching my own memory.

Terry didn't even have to think. "The day he sat down with me outside by the pool and hugged me while I cried about my mother and father's divorce. No one else would let me talk about it. I was hurting, and he could feel it. He cried with me that day. I thought you knew."

I looked at Terry, and a tear rolled down my cheek as long-forgotten memories cascaded into my consciousness.

When I was three, another dog killed my puppy, and my father was there to hold me and teach me what happens when our pets die. When I was five, my father took me to my first day of school. I was so scared. So was he. We cried that first day. The next day he became a teacher's helper.

When I was eight, I just couldn't do math. Father sat down with me every night and we worked until math became easy for me. When I was ten, my father bought me a brand-new bike. When it was stolen because I didn't lock it up, my father gave me jobs around the house so I could earn enough money for another one.

When I was thirteen and my first love broke up with me, my father was there to yell at, to blame, and to cry with. When I was fifteen and got to be in the honor society, my father was there to see me get the accolade. Now, when I was seventeen, he put up with me no matter how nasty I became or how high my hormones raged.

As I looked at my father dancing enthusiastically with my friends, a big toothy grin on his face, I suddenly saw him differently. The handicaps weren't his—they were mine! I had spent much of my life hating the man who loved me. I had hated the exterior and ignored the interior that contained his God-given heart. I felt ashamed.

I asked Terry to take me home, too overcome with feelings to remain.

On graduation day, I stood behind the podium as the valedictorian of my class. As I looked over the audience, my gaze rested on my father in the front row. He sat in his only specially made suit, holding my mother's hand and smiling.

I was overcome with emotion as I began my speech. "Today I stand here as an honor student, able to graduate with a 4.0 average. I didn't do it alone. God was there, and I had friends, teachers, and counselors who helped. If I were to thank just them, I would leave out the most important person in my life: my father."

I saw the look of complete shock cover my father's face. I motioned for him to join me onstage. He made his way slowly, awkwardly, and deliberately. He had to drag his left foot up the stairs as he used his deformed right arm to balance his gait. As he stood next to me at the podium, I took his small, crippled hand in mine and held it tight.

"Sometimes we only see the silhouette of the people around us," I said. "For years I was as shallow as the silhouettes I saw. I saw my father as someone to make fun of, someone to blame, and someone to be ashamed of. He wasn't perfect, like the fathers my friends had.

"Three weeks ago, I found out that while I was envying

my friends' fathers, my friends were envying mine. That made me look at who I was and what I had become."

Then I turned to face my father.

"Father, I owe you a big apology. I based my love for you on what I saw and not what I felt. I forgot to look at the one part of you that meant the most, the big, big heart God gave you. As I move out of high school and into life, I want you to know I could not have had a better father. You were always there for me, and no matter how badly I hurt you, you still showed up. Thank you!"

I took off my mortarboard and placed it on his head.

"You are the reason I am standing here. You deserve this honor, not me."

And as the audience applauded and cried with us, I felt God's light shining upon me as I embraced my father more warmly than I ever had before, tears unashamedly falling down both our faces.

For the first time, I saw my father through God's eyes, and I felt honored to be seen with him.

Love's Power
by Harry Randles, Hot Springs Village, Arkansas

Does Mom hear that train whistle? Pam wondered. Her mother and grandmother were arguing in the front seat of the car. Pam's mom had been cross all morning. *I'd better not say anything,* Pam thought.

As the noise got louder, Pam could see the locomotive barreling toward the crossing. Her mother, oblivious to the danger, hadn't even slowed. "Mom!" she cried.

"In a minute," her mother snapped.

Pam screamed, "Mom, look!"

It was too late. The train cleanly sheared off the front seat of the car. Pam and her sister were left unhurt in the backseat as their mother and grandmother were ground beneath the train for a full quarter of a mile down the track.

The eighth-grader returning to school that fall was not the same girl who had left. In seventh grade, Pam had been a student whom teachers enjoyed. Bright and eager to learn, she had never been a discipline problem. But that Pam had ceased to exist. The Pam who came back to school in September was sullen, angry, inattentive, and difficult to have around. She was

frequently disciplined for her rudeness and disrespectful
behavior. She was obviously very troubled.

Pam's guidance counselor, Rose, worried about Pam. Rose
was usually successful at reaching troubled kids, but weeks
passed, and her frustration grew. Ken, Pam's science teacher,
also was frustrated. He couldn't get through Pam's shell. The
three of us met frequently to discuss her. By November, her
behavior had worsened. All of us were worried but felt our
hands were tied. It is difficult to reach out to a student without being accused of indiscretion or even perversion.

The week after Thanksgiving, Ken showed me a newspaper article and picture of his high school science teacher who
was retiring. The article traced the life of this man who had
mentored and inspired Ken. After reading the article, Ken
decided to meet with Pam and discuss personal feelings,
regardless of the political incorrectness of doing so.

"I can't help but wonder where I'd be today if Mr.
Smith hadn't reached out to me," Ken fumed. "I am so sick
of walking on eggshells when kids need help!"

At the end of science class one day, Ken gave Pam a
note for her study-hall teacher requesting that Pam come
to see him that afternoon. Pam entered the room with a
big chip securely fastened on her shoulder, expecting to be
reprimanded for some new transgression. She slumped into
a seat. Ken moved a chair next to her and opened a folder
full of photos.

"This," he said, "is my mother. I love her. She's always been there for me. I can't even imagine my life without her. It must be hard for you." When Pam just looked away, he moved to the next picture, his mentor. He told her that without his mentor, he would not be who he is today. "He was a great teacher," Ken said. "He inspired me. I loved him, too. But it was a different kind of love than I have for my mom."

More pictures filled the folder: one of Ken's two little girls and his wife, and one of Christ. He expressed his love for his family as he talked with Pam. The picture of Jesus prompted him to explain how he loved the Lord and how that love differed from any earthly love. Pointing to those pictures, he said, "All of these are people I love."

The final picture in the file was of Pam. He gently said, "This is someone else I love. I know it's awkward for a teacher to tell a student this. But what happened last summer convinces me that you should know." Tears sparkled on Pam's lashes. "You're a terrific person. I love you for that. And I love you for your love of learning and many, many other things. And I love you unconditionally."

Tears streamed down Pam's cheeks. It was the first time Ken had seen anything but anger from her in a long time. Ken retrieved a box of tissues from the front of the room and slid it to her. They sat quietly until she was ready to leave.

The change in Pam began that afternoon. Day by day, week by week, she began to gain ground. Rose, Ken, and I watched with delight as she progressed. By Easter she was nearly the delightful girl she had been before that traumatic accident. I was convinced the power of Ken's love inspired Pam's journey back to her former self.

Rose didn't agree. She believed it was the Holy Spirit's power moving through Ken that inspired him to share his feelings with Pam, and thus heal her. Only God knows for sure, as He smiles down on a living photo album of the children He loves.

A Sign from God
by Sara Jordan, Limestone, Maine

I was having a particularly frustrating day, and now I was stuck in traffic. I raised my eyes to heaven and asked, "Why, Lord?"

Then the billboard caught my eye. It was black and white with simple lettering: "WE NEED TO TALK. —GOD."

I looked twice to be sure I'd read it correctly. A billboard from God?

How timely!

I have spent my life trying to attain the patience of Job, the wisdom of Solomon, and the faith of Abraham. But too often, I fall short—ending up the doubting Thomas. And at this point in my life, as I looked at that billboard, I thought with a tinge of bitterness, *Yes, Lord, You're right. We do need to talk.*

We need to talk about why, when I've prayed so hard and so long, You took our two babies through miscarriage. With so many unwanted, abused, and neglected children in the world, why were mine not given the chance to live? Why was I given Graves' disease? Why are we still struggling to have children? Why, why, why?

My faith had been shaken to its very foundation. I needed to reconnect with God, and that billboard spurred me to revisit my relationship with my creator. We "talked" for quite some time.

Through the rest of my week, I wondered about the billboard. I could see no sponsors listed. I assumed some church was "advertising" for souls. But that weekend, when I was in the car with my husband, David, I had a change in attitude.

We were driving down the interstate at a good clip when I saw another black billboard with simple white lettering that asked: "NEED DIRECTIONS? —GOD."

"Dave, look. Another sign from God!" I shouted.

He was so startled he nearly drove off the road. "For heaven's sake," he said, "don't do that!"

He craned his neck to see what I was talking about. "Oh yeah. I see it. I was expecting the sky to open up and angels to appear when you said it was a sign from God!"

We laughed and discussed the sign, and then we became lost in our own thoughts again. I thought, *Maybe God does give us "signs" along the way. Maybe even in the form of billboards. Who knows? It could be His way of giving us a nudge in the right direction.*

And, I thought, *I do need directions, Lord. Guide me.*

From then on, I began to look for those "signs from God." I found seventeen in locations from country roads to busy highways. "REMEMBER THAT LOVE THY NEIGHBOR THING? I MEANT IT." "IF YOU KEEP TAKING MY NAME IN VAIN, I'LL MAKE RUSH HOUR LONGER." All of them were signed "GOD."

The signs spoke to me when I seemed to need answers or encouragement the most. *Maybe God has a hand in this,* I acknowledged, *and He's trying to tell me something.*

That became apparent in the middle of a heated discussion between Dave and me. The loss of our unborn children and the subsequent financial and emotional strain of infertility treatment were taking their toll on our relationship. I was disillusioned with prayer and love. We were arguing in the car when we passed a sign that was surely meant for us: "LOVED THE WEDDING. NOW INVITE ME TO THE MARRIAGE. —GOD."

It stopped us cold. The sign reminded us of where we should turn for strength to keep on going. God had brought us together, and, for whatever reason, He was allowing this grief in our lives. He would get us through it if we would turn to Him. It was a pivotal moment for us.

When you want something with all of your heart, it's difficult to release those dreams and let God direct your life. The hardest lesson I had to learn is that God's will is not always my will. I know, though, that I can rest in the knowledge that God has a plan for me, and that eventually, all will be revealed.

I never learned who erected those billboards. They are gradually being replaced with the usual billboard fare of commercial ads. I'm sorry to see them go. I hope others gained as much from their messages as I did. Maybe other lives were as forever changed as mine. Now, whenever I'm discouraged or disgusted with life, I remember one sign in particular:

"I LOVE YOU. . .

"I LOVE YOU. . .

"I LOVE YOU. . .

"—GOD"

The Wedding
by John P. Walker, New Cumberland, Pennsylvania

Jack and Jean were among our first friends when I began ministry in my first full-time pastorate. Their friendly faces and warm smiles encouraged a young preacher with the Sunday morning pulpit jitters. I was surprised that their smiles were genuine—they had been through more trials than almost anyone I had ever known.

Jack had been a chemist until a severe form of rheumatoid arthritis took him from being a healthy worker to someone confined to a wheelchair and living on disability. By the time I met him, he could barely move from the wheelchair, and then only to shift to another chair or to stand for a moment. Pain filled his face as he made these rare transitions.

He and Jean got around well in a new van converted for the wheelchair. A small elevator installed in their townhouse moved Jack between the floors. And despite his misshapen, arthritis-bent fingers, Jack learned to use a computer and helped us at the church with financial work.

I wasn't surprised when Susan, Jack and Jean's daughter, asked me to officiate at her wedding. Her father had hinted that this might be coming.

One day before the wedding, Susan stopped at my office. From her expression, I knew something was seriously wrong. "My dad wants to walk me down the aisle," she said, close to tears. "He thinks he can do it. He insists on it."

The next day, while he sat at his kitchen table drinking tea, Jack adamantly told me, "I'll practice until the wedding. I'm going to do this. Please pray for me!" I knew no one could change Jack's mind when he was determined to do something, so I let the subject drop. I did, however, pray.

At the wedding rehearsal, we discussed several scenarios that would allow Jack to "present" the bride. Only one of the three involved his walking down the aisle, and we included that option only to please Jack. A brief experiment seemed to deflate Jack's determination as he took only a few steps before he had to sit back down. From the platform, I watched sadly as he hung his head. Again, I prayed.

On the wedding day, everything proceeded as planned. I stood on the steps of the platform with groom and groomsmen, awaiting the bridal party. The music played, and the bridesmaids walked down the aisle. As the maid of honor stepped into position, the organist paused and played the dramatic opening notes of "The Wedding March."

I thought about Jack. He had been brought to the sanctuary steps earlier and now waited in his wheelchair by the door. With the struggles of the previous evening still in mind, Jack would not be walking the aisle today. I was disappointed for his sake, and I couldn't imagine his pain. This had meant so much to him.

The bride had to walk from the side of the sanctuary behind the last row of pews before turning into the center aisle. I could barely see the tuft of Susan's white tulle veil above the heads of the now-standing congregation.

I saw that tuft of white stop. Then I heard the hum of murmuring voices begin. The beautiful bride turned into the main aisle. It took a second for me to realize what was happening: Susan was being escorted by her father, who was walking!

Slowly and painfully, Jack took a few steps and then paused to catch his breath. With a cane in his left hand and Susan on his right side, father and daughter moved toward me. The entire congregation seemed to be holding its collective breath, all of us afraid the next step would be the last. I believe, in that moment, we were all praying for Jack.

A few more minutes inched past before the bride and her father finally arrived at the front.

Still awestruck, I voiced a shaky introduction and almost choked up when I asked, "Who presents this woman to be married to this man?"

Jack's voice rang out strong and proud, "Her mother and I do."

Susan hugged her father and took her place beside her

husband-to-be. I noticed her face was wet with tears. I realized my own face was wet! In fact, it seemed the whole congregation had been deeply moved.

The wedding reception was wonderful. It was one of the grandest I had ever attended. But whatever the excitement of the celebration, the highlight of the day was the miracle we had witnessed: the miracle of Jack, with determination born of love and faith in the living God, escorting his daughter down the aisle on her wedding day!

No truer words express the miracle of that than as those in Mark 10:27: " 'With man this is impossible, but not with God; all things are possible with God.' "

Daddy Hands
by Susan Farr Fahncke, Kaysville, Utah

I awoke in the night to find my husband, Marty, gently rocking our baby, Noah. I stood unnoticed in the doorway, watching this amazing man. He lovingly stroked Noah's fat little cheeks, trying to comfort him. I watched as my husband moved Noah's cheek against his own chest so Noah could feel the vibrations of his voice.

Noah is deaf. Learning to comfort him has been a whole new experience for us. We relied on our voices, audio toys, and music for our other children, but with Noah, we use touch, sight, the "feel" of our voices, and sign language to communicate with him and comfort him.

My husband made the sign for "I love you" with his hand. A tear rolled down his cheek as he placed Noah's weak hand on top of his own. For a week and a half, Noah's fever had been high and dangerous despite everything the doctor had tried. When I touched my husband's shoulder, we looked at each other. We both feared that Noah wasn't getting any better. I offered to take over for Marty, but he shook his head. Many men would have gladly handed over the parenting duties for some much-needed sleep, but Marty resolutely stayed with his child.

When morning came, we took Noah to the doctor's office. Our hearts were filled with dread as the doctor told us Noah needed to be admitted to a hospital. Now.

Our experience in the hospital was torturous. Noah's screams echoed through the halls as he endured the horrible tests. Marty reassured me that he felt in his heart that Noah would be okay. He never wavered. He comforted me, Noah, and everyone who called to check on Noah. Marty was a rock.

When the first batch of tests was completed, a nurse told us a spinal tap might be necessary because the doctors suspected meningitis. Marty and I prayed together. With tears streaming down his face, my husband lifted his voice to the Lord. As he humbly asked for the Lord to heal our son, my heart filled with comfort. Marty's prayer was speedily answered. A short time later, the doctor came in to tell us that Noah had Influenza A. No spinal tap would be needed, and the doctor felt that Noah would soon be back to his old zesty self.

A few days after Noah was released from the hospital, I was cooking dinner when I peeked into the living room. I chuckled at the picture I saw. Marty was sitting in his "daddy chair," with Noah in his lap. They were reading a book. Marty would take Noah's teeny hands and help him form the signs for the words. They caught me watching them. My husband and I simultaneously signed "I love you" to each other, then to Noah. And then Noah put his little arm up, trying to shape his chubby hand in his own effort to sign "I love you" to his daddy. I watched with tears as my husband carefully helped Noah form his tiny fingers into the sign with his own gentle hands.

Daddy hands.

Handcrafted with Love
by Lanita Bradley Boyd, Fort Thomas, Kentucky

"This smoke is more than I can bear!" Mom whispered, exasperated. "Having my blood taken twice a day and enduring chemotherapy is bad enough without choking on her cigarette smoke!"

I knew my mother-in-law never wanted to bother the nurses, with whom she was a favorite. Most of them had received her handmade crafts and enjoyed her pleasant spirit. But Mom soon admitted her distress to her nurse and was quickly moved to another room. Moving her myriad of cards, flowers, and craft projects was quite a task.

Then she glimpsed her new roommate. She turned to me, eyes wide. "She's colored!" she whispered, and I winced. I was always amazed that this lovely Christian woman could be so racially intolerant.

The next night the whispered remarks were favorable. "She's ninety-four," Mom informed me. "Had surgery. Her granddaughter has been here all day, and now that's her son and her great-granddaughter. They're nice and so concerned about her. I think she's a religious woman, too."

So far, so good, I thought. Knowing that Mom's cancer was

terminal, I felt confident that she was at peace with the Lord, but I was concerned about her prejudice. Perhaps this would work out well.

It did. Mrs. Lyles was gentle and gracious. Mom greatly respected her.

Then one day Dad came home, head drooping. "Dorothy's roommate left today, and the new one arrived right before I left. I'm afraid Dorothy will have a hard time adjusting—she's African-American and she smokes!"

Lord, why can't You give her roommates who won't upset her? I prayed. How little I knew of His great plan! God's plan became encapsulated in one word: Charlotte.

I couldn't visit Mom that night and hesitantly entered the room the next evening. She was smiling, and the curtains separating the beds were open. I noticed that Charlotte was not much older than I was.

"I want you to meet Charlotte," Mom said, bubbling. She couldn't quit talking about all they had in common. They'd found their lumps at about the same time, each had had the same breast removed, and each was fighting the cancer with every ounce of will possible. Differences in skin color, age, cultural background, children, and religion were irrelevant.

Charlotte's personality complemented Mom's. While Mom could be talkative only if she knew someone well, Charlotte's beautiful smile and loving attitude welcomed everyone as an instant friend. Her dark skin and hair contrasted with Mom's pale face and smooth white hair, but in spirit they were the same.

Charlotte felt she had no creative skills and loved every item Mom made. She seemed to sense Mom's needs for reassurance and physical assistance and always said and did just the right thing. At that time, Charlotte could move more easily about the room, so she would get Mom a drink or pick up something that had fallen from the bed. Every time I arrived, they seemed to be laughing about something, though I knew they also had serious moments. As far as Mom and Charlotte were concerned, white and black didn't exist. They were sisters in the deepest sense, sharing the same pain, with the same faith, fears, and hope that chemotherapy would perform some miracle.

After a few days of observing this glowing relationship, I brought up the unmentionable.

"Mom," I asked, "does Charlotte smoke?"

"Oh, sometimes," she replied casually, "but she stands by the window and blows the smoke outside."

Charlotte loved Mom and would have done anything to please her. I knew it was hard for her to smoke less than usual, but she limited her cigarettes as much as possible, taking just a few puffs and then extinguishing her cigarette quickly.

After that chemotherapy round ended, they were on similar return cycles for a while. Even though they were no longer roommates, they visited each other's rooms when their hospital stays coincided. In between, Mom wrote letters to Charlotte, and Charlotte made long telephone calls to Mom. They sympathized and joked about their hair loss and other distressing side effects, making it all more bearable for each other.

One day, as Mom waited to see if her blood count was high enough to be admitted for chemotherapy, she peered around the room and down the hall, hoping to see Charlotte, who also had an appointment that day. She clutched the newest doll she had exhaustingly made to give Charlotte.

At the moment the nurse called Mom's name, Charlotte was wheeled into the elevator.

"Just a minute!" Mom said to the nurse as she tottered to the elevator. Mom laid the doll in Charlotte's emaciated lap and leaned over to hug Charlotte's fragile body.

"I love you, Charlotte," she said softly.

"I love you, too, Dorothy," Charlotte answered, squeezing Mom as tightly as she could. They smiled at each other as the elevator door closed.

Mom found out that Charlotte's blood count was now too low for further chemotherapy. She began calling Charlotte daily. By the time Mom returned for her next checkup, Charlotte had been admitted to the hospital. Officially, Charlotte was not allowed company, but Mom persuaded the nurses she knew to gain entry anyway.

As Mom held her friend's hand for the last time, she

was grateful that Charlotte recognized her.

Charlotte's husband called the next day to say that Charlotte had died that night. Mom, though tearful, took it calmly.

"We both knew we didn't have long. She was so young, I just didn't think that she'd be the first to go," Mom said. "But I could see that she was always just a little further along than I was."

In only a few weeks, Mom was gone, too. Even in our grief, we could accept her passing more easily, because we knew that through God's grace, Mom had overcome her bigotry. God had given Mom the opportunity to learn that love and friendship are based not on outward appearances but on the heart.

The Garden
by Alex and Dawn Edwards, Aurora, Illinois

Carl didn't talk much. He would always greet people with a big smile and a firm handshake, but even after Carl had lived in our neighborhood for more than fifty years, no one could say that they knew him well. All we really knew was that he had worked for the gas company and that when he retired, he'd won an award for never having taken a sick day in fifty-one years with the company.

Before his retirement, Carl took the bus to work each morning. As his retirement approached and he grew older, the sight of him walking down the street alone often worried us. He had a slight limp from a bullet wound received in World War II. The bullet was still lodged very near his spine. We worried that although he had survived World War II, he might not make it through our changing uptown neighborhood with its increasing violence, gangs, and drug activity.

Carl was in his early seventies when he began what was to be more than fifteen years of caring for the gardens behind the minister's residence. His wife had been dead for a few years when he saw the flyer at our local church asking for volunteers. Without fanfare, he signed up to do the weeding, watering, and seeding of flowers and vegetables that were planted each spring.

He was well into his eighty-seventh year when the thing we had always feared finally happened. He was just finishing his watering for the day when three gang members approached him. Ignoring their attempt to intimidate him, he simply asked, "Would you like a drink from the hose?"

The tallest and toughest-looking said, "Yeah, sure," with a malevolent smile. As Carl offered the hose to him, the other two grabbed Carl's arms, throwing him down. As the hose snaked crazily over the ground, dousing everything in its path, Carl's assailants stole his retirement watch and his wallet and then fled.

Carl tried to get up, but he had been thrown down on his bad leg. He lay there trying to gather himself as the minister came running to help him. The minister had witnessed the attack from his window but couldn't get there fast enough to stop it. "Carl, are you okay? Are you hurt?" the minister asked as he helped Carl to his feet.

Carl passed a hand over his brow and sighed, shaking his head. "Just some punk kids. I hope they'll wise up someday." His wet clothes clung to his slight frame as he picked up the hose and resumed watering.

Concerned, the minister asked, "Carl, what are you doing?"

"I've got to finish my watering. It's been very dry

lately," Carl calmly replied. Satisfying himself that Carl really was all right, the minister could only marvel.

A few weeks later, the three returned. Carl again offered them a drink. This time they didn't rob him. They wrenched the hose from his hand and drenched him in the icy water as he tried to fend them off. When they finished humiliating him, they sauntered down the street, catcalling and cursing, falling over one another with laughter. Carl just watched them. Then he turned toward the warm sun, picked up his hose, and continued watering.

The summer was quickly fading into fall. Carl was tilling and getting the rose beds ready for their winter mulch protection when he was startled by someone approaching him from behind. He stumbled and fell into some evergreen branches. As he struggled to regain his footing, he saw the leader of his summer tormentors reaching for him. He braced himself for the expected attack.

"Don't worry, old man. I'm not gonna hurt you this time." The young man spoke softly, still offering the tattooed hand to Carl. Then he pulled a crumpled bag from his pocket and handed it to Carl.

"What's this?" Carl asked.

"It's your stuff," the young man explained. "Even the money in your wallet."

"I don't understand," Carl said. "Why would you help me now?"

The young man shifted his feet, seeming embarrassed and ill at ease.

"I learned something from you," he said. "I ran with that gang and hurt people like you. We picked you because you were old, and we knew we could do it. But every time we did something to you, instead of yelling and fighting back, you tried to give us a drink. You didn't hate us for hating you. You kept showing love against our hate." He stopped for a moment. "I couldn't sleep after we stole your stuff, so here it is back." He paused for another awkward moment. "That bag's my way of saying thanks for straightening me out, I guess." And with that, he walked down the street.

Carl gingerly opened the bag in his hands. He took out his retirement watch and put it back on his wrist. Opening his wallet, he checked for his wedding photo. He gazed for a moment at the young bride who still smiled back at him from all those years ago. He pocketed his billfold once again and went back to mulching his roses.

Carl didn't make it to the following spring to see those roses bloom again. He died one cold day after Christmas. Many people attended his funeral, in spite of the weather. The minister noticed a tall young man sitting quietly in a corner of the church. The minister spoke of Carl's garden as a lesson in life. In a voice thick with unshed tears, he said, "Do your best and make your garden as beautiful as you can. We will never forget Carl and his garden."

That spring, as the ice thawed in the yard, another flyer went up: PERSON NEEDED TO CARE FOR CARL'S GARDEN. No one seemed to notice the flyer until one day when someone knocked on the minister's office door. Opening the door, the minister saw a pair of tattooed hands holding the flyer.

"I believe this is my job, if you'll have me," the young man said. The minister recognized him as the same young man who had returned the stolen watch and wallet to Carl. He knew Carl's kindness had turned this man's life around. As the minister handed him the keys to the garden shed, he said, "Yes, go take care of Carl's garden and honor him."

Over the next several years, the young man tended the flowers and vegetables just as Carl had done. In that time, he went to college, got married, and became a prominent businessman. But he never forgot his promise to Carl's memory and kept the garden as beautiful as he thought Carl would have kept it.

One day he approached the new minister and told him that he couldn't care for the garden any longer. He explained with a shy and happy smile, "My wife just had our baby last night, and she's coming home Saturday."

"Well, congratulations!" said the minister as he took the garden shed keys. "That's wonderful! What's the baby's name?"

It was Carl.

I Remember

by Pat Toornman Bales, Brighton, Colorado

"Quick, John, run inside the house and get a bunch of bath towels," James commanded. "Call Frankie now, and tell him to hurry! Joseph, hold the hind legs as tightly as you can. Mom, Frankie told me what to do. I've read books, and I know I can do it. Quit worrying."

James tried to calm me, but those words, coming from a twelve-year-old boy, were anything but reassuring.

A ewe had had a rupture during pregnancy. Torn muscles in her side prevented her lamb from entering the birth canal. Knowing she couldn't have a normal delivery, I had wanted to get rid of her, but my oldest son, James, insisted that he could handle her and her pregnancy and that he could operate when the time came.

I was not ready for this. Struggling to keep the farm after my husband left, working, and trying to raise the boys by myself had taken a toll. I thought I was independent. I believed my faith was strong. Now, circumstances tested all that confidence.

My boys had grown up fast when their dad stepped out of our lives. Everything we had taken for granted was gone. Our world had been turned upside down. We owned the farm and animals, but I didn't have a full-time job. Counting pennies to buy a gallon of milk became common. Even though my boys were helpful, they were still young. The daily problems—and we had many—rested on my shoulders. Emotionally, we were all drained.

I remembered the first time I felt all alone. One day during the second year of my marriage, my neighbor Sharon found me crying. I was pregnant with James and unhappy with my marriage. As I sobbed, she held me and dried my tears. Then she prayed with me. Sharon explained that the God I vaguely knew as a child was there for me every moment of every day. I started attending church, reading my Bible, and building my relationship with Him daily. God used that time to change me. Whenever I became frightened, I could remember God loved me, and I was not alone. I would pray, and it quieted my fears.

But there were still times like this when I felt overwhelmed. I forgot the promise that He would always be with me. I was depending on myself and barely surviving. I needed to depend on Him. When I prayed, peace flooded over me. I could get that same peace now, if only I asked Him. Closing my eyes, I tried it.

My body rigid with tension, I prayed silently, "God, You're in control. You know I can't do this alone. I keep trying, but I just can't do it by myself anymore. . . . Please help me. . . . Please show me Your love. I need You."

The prayer calmed my quaking body.

Eight-year-old John returned with a stack of towels. "Frankie's on his way. He said James knows how to get her ready and that the timing is *real important*."

"James, what does he mean by that?" I asked.

"Mom, just grab her front legs and hold them apart and steady." James's voice was a whisper, but it was braced with control. My grip held steady.

"John, help Joseph hold her back legs, 'cause she'll start kicking."

With methodical precision, James cut the ewe's belly. Joseph and John held tightly to her back legs. Opening my eyes, looking at my three young sons' faces, I saw something I hadn't noticed before. John and Joseph were looking at James with complete faith and following orders. James looked at me with a determination well beyond his twelve years. I knew we were going to make it.

"I feel the lamb! I think I got it! John, hold both legs! Joseph, grab a towel!"

James pulled out a wet, wiggly lamb still attached to its mother and handed it to Joseph. We all felt triumphant as James cut the cord. Joseph, only six years old, started rubbing the lamb dry.

"Hey, James, how's it going?" boomed Frankie as he strode into the barn.

"Look, it's alive! We have a baby!" James squealed,

sounding more like a boy of twelve than the confident young man I had just watched deliver a lamb.

"Remember, there are usually more than one. Twins are the norm," Frankie said.

"Here, you take over." James started to move to the side of the ewe.

"No way, young man. You started it; you can finish it. I'll take John's place, and he can take care of the next lamb."

During the next ten minutes, James found not just twins, but triplets! All three were given to John and Joseph who dried them off and carried them into the house.

Those lambs are grown and gone. Joseph and John are now teenagers. James just finished his junior year at the Air Force Academy and is applying to medical schools. He wants to be a doctor. It is a dream he has had since he was twelve.

When I asked him what made him choose a career in medicine, he answered, "Mom, do you remember the day our ewe ruptured, and I had to deliver triplets? That day I knew what I wanted to do with my life. I felt God there with me."

I looked at him, and I did remember. I remember that day and my boys' expressions as clearly as if it were yesterday. I also remember other days that have come and gone and how thankful I am for them. Most of all, I remember I am not alone. I always have a friend, someone who loves me and helps carry my everyday worries and concerns—just as He did the day James delivered triplet lambs.

Michelle
by Tracy Bohannon, Riverview, Florida

Michelle came to us at the age of two as our first foster child. As I looked at her for the first time, I prayed, "God, please let this work out."

She had shoulder-length, wispy brown hair and the saddest blue eyes I had ever seen. I hoped we were up to the challenge of parenting a foster child. We had attended a class for prospective foster parents, which was supposed to teach us everything we would need to know. What the class couldn't teach us was the incredible love we would experience.

Gradually, Michelle's eyes went from being sorrowful to sparkling with mischief, like any other toddler's. We all adored her, especially our four-year-old son. Michelle opened our eyes to simple joys that we had always taken for granted.

Michelle showed us that a walk in the park was much more than a simple pleasure—it was a way to connect, to be one with God's creations. Holding Michelle's hand in one of mine and my son's hand in the other, I marveled at the simple but powerful act of love and protectiveness in holding just one small hand.

Then one night, after the children were in bed, we received

a telephone call. A relative was willing to take Michelle. Although we had known that a foster child could leave at any time, we were completely unprepared. I climbed the stairs as Michelle slept and quietly packed her things. The next day, her social worker arrived promptly at ten. I carried Michelle out, and after a long hug and a kiss, followed by many tears, I placed her in the car and watched her leave.

To have had the privilege of loving her was a miracle granted to us from God. We learned so much from this very special little girl. She paved the way for all the children who would follow her. We were able to love and cherish each child who came to us, no matter what the circumstance. Most important, we learned how to let go, no matter how painful it might be. With God's help, we tried to love them as Jesus loves us—unconditionally and with a steadfast love.

Although we don't see Michelle anymore, we continue to feel the love she gave and the changes she brought to our family. She will always be a part of our hearts, reminding us of the blessings that are ours every day.

"Make a Wish, Mommy"
by Susan Farr Fahncke, Kaysville, Utah

The day before my twenty-eighth birthday, I was depressed. I was used to celebrating my birthday with the friends I had moved away from. I was used to presents and phone calls, but now that I was divorced and raising two children alone, I couldn't even afford a telephone.

I hadn't lived in Utah very long and was still trying to adjust to the snow. This particular January was brutal. The snow outside was thigh-high, and leaving the house was a daily struggle, adding to my isolation. My son, Nicholas, was in kindergarten, and I was a junior at a nearby university. I had taken the quarter off because my baby, Maya, had been very ill. I had no social life and couldn't even remember the happy, laughing person I used to be.

Tucking the children into bed that night, I was in a cloud of hopelessness. Little Nick wrapped his chubby six-year-old arms around my neck and said, "Tomorrow's your birthday, Mommy! I can't wait!" His blue eyes sparkled with anticipation.

Kissing his sweet rosy cheeks, I hoped he didn't expect a birthday party to appear magically, like it did on his birthday.

Life is so simple when you're six.

The next morning, I awoke before the children and began making breakfast. Hearing noises in our tiny living room, I assumed Nick was up and waited for him to come in to eat. Then I could hear Nick talking to Maya. He was sternly telling her to make Mommy smile today.

It suddenly hit me. Wrapped up in my misery, I didn't see how it was affecting my children. Even my little boy sensed I wasn't happy and was doing his best to help. Tears of shame washed down my face. I knelt in our little kitchen and asked for the strength to find happiness again. I asked God to show me some beauty in my life. I asked Him to help me really see the blessings I did have.

Putting a smile on my face, I marched into the living room to hug my children. Nick sat on the floor with Maya. In front of them was a pile of presents. A birthday party for three.

I looked at the presents. Then my disbelieving eyes went back to my son. "I surprised you, Mommy, didn't I? Happy birthday!" He grinned his toothless, adorable grin.

Stunned, I knelt next to him and asked him how he had found a way to get me presents. He reminded me of our trip to the dollar store. I remembered him telling me he was spending the allowance he had been saving. I had laughed at his bulging pockets and remembered thinking that he walked like John Wayne with his pants loaded like that. I had almost chided him for spending everything he had so carefully saved but decided not to.

Looking again at the beautiful pile of presents in front of me, I couldn't believe that my small, darling son had spent everything in his bank on *me*. What kind of kid goes without the toys he wanted so he could buy his *mom* a pile of presents?

There in the living room, I heard a voice in my heart say, *I am showing you your blessings. How could you ever doubt them?*

My prayers were being answered. No one had more to be thankful for than I did. With tears flowing, I hugged my son and daughter. I carefully opened each present. A bracelet. A necklace. Another bracelet. Nail polish. Another bracelet. My favorite candy bars. Another bracelet. The thoughtful gifts— each wrapped in gift bags and wrapping paper also purchased with Nick's allowance—were perfect.

The final gift was Nick's favorite—a wax birthday cake with the words "I love you" painted in fake frosting across the top. "You have to have a birthday cake, Mom," my little one informed me.

"It's the most beautiful cake I've ever seen," I told him, and it was.

Then he sang "Happy Birthday" to me in his sweet little-boy voice. "Make a wish, Mommy," he insisted.

I looked into my little boy's shining blue eyes and couldn't think of a single thing I would wish for.

"I've already got my wish," I whispered. "I have you."

Bathroom Blessing
by Malinda Fillingim, Roanoke Rapids, North Carolina

Whatever else can be said of me, I cry well. During the four months that my daughter, Hope, was in the hospital, crying became a habit. I tried to be strong for her sake. I bravely held her hand and reassured her that everything was going to be okay—even when I really wasn't so certain of that myself.

One afternoon, I was completely worn out and needed a break. I needed a quiet place to pray. I needed a place where I could break down and no one would notice. The only place I could find was the large bathroom off the lobby. There, I locked the bathroom stall door and began to cry.

My sobs echoed throughout the tile-floored room. I blew my nose on toilet paper and flushed the toilet, hoping the sound would drown out my weeping. After a few minutes, feet began to appear, one pair after another, under my locked door. I began to hear voices.

"Are you okay in there?" a woman asked. Another woman slid a cold paper towel under my door. "Whatever is wrong, honey, I am going to pray for you. It'll be okay." A teenager rolled her unopened can of soda to me. I thanked her and drank it. Two women offered to wait for me outside in the hall and pray with me. Another young woman with two small children told me she was sorry for whatever was wrong. Many people shared words of comfort. One person even sang "Amazing Grace" to me!

My bathroom stall became a holy place where my sorrow was shared by strangers who comforted me, sight unseen. Except for feet, of course.

I finished my crying. The tears had cleansed my soul, and strangers had buoyed my spirit. As I walked back to Hope's room, a woman asked how I was feeling. When I asked how she knew me, she laughed and said, "I recognized your shoes!" Looking down, I recognized hers, too. We hugged.

Returning to Hope's room, I looked at our situation with new faith and with the reassurance that I was not alone. God had spoken to me through the kindness of strangers.

A bathroom stall may not have a lot of room, but it is plenty big enough for God to work wonders and help our perspective on life take a U-turn.

Love First, Teach Second
by Joan Clayton, Portales, New Mexico

"You're going to have Mary in your room?" a fellow teacher asked apprehensively. "I feel sorry for you!"

"She's on medication, you know," another teacher warned. "You will be, too, before the year's over!"

I had heard similar comments during eighteen years of teaching. But usually all of my first-grade children turned out to be normal. So I began the year with calm assurance that I could handle whatever came. Was I in for a surprise!

A few days before school started, Mary and her mother dropped by to "get acquainted." Golden blond hair cascaded perfectly down the little girl's back. Large, beautiful blue eyes gazed into mine. As her mother and I talked, Mary interrupted us with her outbursts. I learned that Mary needed medication for hyperactivity and asthma. The office would keep the medicine, and I would send Mary for it every day after lunch.

Then came the first day of school.

Purses, tablets, marking pens, hair barrettes, gimmicks of all kinds—Mary dropped the whole assortment as she bounced into the room. Every time I turned around, some child was crawling under a table to retrieve Mary's loot.

Mary didn't seem able to whisper. She frequently blurted out comments, disturbing the entire class. "The answer is ahh. . .one. *No*, two. . .no, threee."

Scrubbing vigorously with her eraser, she usually tore the paper and would start the whole procedure with a fresh sheet of paper again and again.

One day I told the office secretary, "Mary's medication doesn't seem to help."

"What medication?" the secretary asked. "She hasn't been in for it since school started."

After that, I began sending another child with her to see that she took her pill. Even as she resumed her daily medication, I still had to deal with Mary's frequent outbursts.

One day, after constantly shushing, isolating, and reprimanding Mary, I said, "All right, Mary, come to the front. Take all the time you need to talk, wiggle, or whatever so you can settle down and we can get back to work."

This drastic method had always worked in my classes before. The student, embarrassed, would stand silently and be happy to sit down and continue working.

But not Mary. At first she jumped up and down, growling like a caged bear. Then she pounded on the desks with her fists, screaming like Tarzan. The children loved the show. This encouraged her to show off even more. After five minutes of these antics, I could stand no more. This little girl had outsmarted me!

In the following weeks, I ran the gamut of rewards, praise, and reinforcing positive behavior (when I could find any). Nothing seemed to work. At the end of one particularly harassing day, I dismissed the children and slumped in my chair, defeated. I had tried everything.

Everything, that is, except prayer!

With my head on my desk, I prayed, "Lord, help me with this child. Show me the key."

I dozed off. When I awakened a few minutes later, my frustration and weariness had disappeared. Two words came to mind: *Love her.*

I thought I already loved her. Yet those two words— "Love her"—lingered. And they were there when I awakened the next morning.

"Lord," I prayed, "I already love her, so I'm going to take those two words to mean that I'm to love her physically."

I hurried to school bursting with anticipation. God had answered, and I was eager to see His plan unfold.

When the bell rang, Mary bounded in with enough energy for the whole class. I gave her paper to write her spelling words on, and she jumped ten frog leaps to her seat. Then she began to write and spell out loud, "D-O-W-N. Deee. . .ohh. . .double-uu. . .enn!"

"Mary, come to my desk, please," I said quietly.

With two hops, a skip, a side two-step, and three giant

steps backward, Mary obeyed my command. Silently, I pulled her toward me and held her close. In my thoughts I was praying, *Lord, help this little child to calm down. Take away whatever is causing her hyperactivity.*

Sometimes these sessions would last five minutes with no one speaking. The other children watched silently and seemed to understand.

If Mary's behavior seemed to be getting out of control, we would stop and hug, while the class waited patiently and lovingly. Sometimes we would do this four or five times a day.

One week later, Mary's reading teacher came running across the hall.

"Whatever has happened to Mary? She isn't the same child!"

"It's called 'pray and hug therapy,'" I explained. "I silently pray for her every day, and before I let her come to the reading class, I stop the children, hug her, and say a silent prayer."

"Well, don't stop!" the teacher exclaimed.

In just a few short weeks, other staff members noticed Mary's behavior change.

I knew in my heart that God was leading.

It is now spring. Last fall seems long ago. It's hard to think of Mary now as ever having had problems. When she raises her hand to answer a question but instead says, "Teacher, I love you," I say a silent prayer of thanksgiving.

In a few minutes the bell will ring, and the children will come in—each with different needs. As I pass out their papers, I pray silently for these little lives that have blessed mine so abundantly.

Lord, bless these children today. Help me always to love first and teach second!

The Gift—Confessions of a Surrogate Mother
by Carrie Mikolajczyk-Russell, Toledo, Ohio

The last time I gave this gift was a wintry day in December 1999. The twins, Ryan and Alexa, came into this world to be received by their parents with all the love hearts can hold. I knew those parents' gratitude would forever hold a place in my heart.

And now I had heard my calling again. The embryo transfer was successful. God had blessed me with the ability to carry yet another child for yet another couple. And the day we'd all waited for so anxiously had arrived.

On the morning of the birth, we all met for breakfast. Tim and Lisa, the parents-to-be, greeted my husband and me with hugs. Tim is a pediatrician and Lisa is an OB-GYN. They had endured years of heartache trying to have a child. But on this day, they felt only excitement and joy for what was about to take place.

On the way to the hospital, my husband held my hand. These moments were very precious to me. They were my final moments with this baby who had touched my heart in so many ways. He had his very own personality, this child who slept with me and woke with me. He made me laugh when he was active. I knew I would miss his presence, as I had missed the twins. But now it was time to close this chapter. It was time to create a family. It was time to help God unite loving parents with their child.

Labor was induced at 1:30 p.m. A short while later, the contractions brought tears to my eyes. Lisa sat next to me expressing her regret for my discomfort. I reminded myself of how small a price it was—I knew she would have given anything to feel each wave of pain. Shortly after five o'clock, I prepared for the first push. I had no idea I had two more agonizing hours of labor ahead.

By 7:00 p.m. I was exhausted, and my doctor looked anxious. Convinced that I could go no further, I felt conflicted. All through my pregnancy, I had prayed each night for the strength and ability to carry this baby to term. Every night I had said to God, "I know I can do this, but not without You." Now, in my darkest, weakest hour, I knew I had to depend on Him. I closed my eyes and prayed. "God, please help me to bring forth this child. I can't do it without You."

The next push was not "the one," and neither was the next. I was not discouraged. I would not lose my faith in my ability to do this, and I began looking forward to the next contraction. When it came, I repeated my prayer. I felt the baby making progress. He was coming!

When I pushed for the last time, everyone shed tears of joy. All that mattered to me now was seeing this woman I had come to love receive her child. I wanted to see a father gaze upon his firstborn son. I wanted to see what I had achieved with God's help.

As Lisa stepped forward to claim her son, he was gently placed in her arms. She cried tears that washed away years of pain and emptiness. Tim had come up behind Lisa with his own tears. They were parents at last.

I thought, *Look at what God chose me to do.* I could feel God was smiling as I looked at Tim and Lisa again. Some people go their entire lives and never get to see what I saw in those moments. I've been blessed with seeing it twice.

So many people ask surrogate mothers, "Why would you do this for someone?"

These moments answer those questions. I have these memories that leave an imprint in my mind, my heart, and my soul that can never be erased.

Two days later I held Harrison for the last time. I told him to always remember how special he is. I told him how proud I was to have been chosen to give him life, and then I said good-bye.

I was filled with satisfaction, and I thanked God once more for my own children and my ability to be a surrogate mother. I walked out of the hospital with my children's hands in mine, fully aware of the gift I clasped in each hand. The sun shone down upon my face, and I looked at everything as if I were seeing it for the first time.

Five Minutes to Live
by Jill Lauritzen Zimanek, Athens, Georgia

"Jill, we're going to pump your stomach; then we'll give you an alcohol drip, which will be like a triple cocktail in an IV. But I have to tell you. . .this could kill you. And if it doesn't, you could go blind or have kidney damage," the doctor said matter-of-factly. Then he gave me five minutes to say good-bye to my family.

Minutes earlier, I had been completely healthy, and now a doctor was saying the sand in my hourglass was running out. . .fast.

We were driving home from our Christmas vacation with family in Pittsburgh, when I accidentally ingested methanol, a chemical so toxic that four teaspoons is fatal. Our windshield wiper fluid had frozen under the hood, so we had put some fluid in a Gatorade bottle to squirt periodically on our windshield. While reading to my husband, I grabbed the wrong Gatorade bottle and chugged down. When I felt the burning in my chest, I realized what I had done. I drank water while my husband got directions to the nearest hospital.

Within minutes, I was explaining to hospital personnel what had happened. Nurses looked at me sympathetically and patted my leg. Then the doctor laid it on the line. While my husband ran to get our children, the nurses inserted a tube through my nose into my stomach.

The children came into the room, crying. The tube made it difficult to speak, but it was harder to know what to say. How could I sum up my feelings for my family in five minutes? I started to cry, which made my throat hurt worse.

"If Mommy dies," I started slowly, "where is she going?"

"To heaven," my daughter said, sobbing.

"That's right," I said slowly. "And where did Mommy say she'd be in heaven?"

"With arms wide open at the gate waiting for us," they said together.

We held hands and held each other as best we could. I took a heart-shaped piece of shell my son had given me years ago at the beach from my purse and held it tightly in my hand.

"See," I said, showing it to them, "I'll have this with me the whole time and be thinking of you." Knowing I could lose my sight at any moment, I studied their faces. I wanted their images to be the last I'd see.

I thought of my mother and father, whom I so desperately wanted to hug. I thought of my sister and brother, my nephews and nieces.

I thought of friends. . . . I would never get to tell them how much they meant to me. I felt ripped apart inside.

Moments later I was taken by ambulance to another hospital, on a continuous alcohol drip. I was the only legal drunk in West Virginia.

My husband had made four telephone calls: one to my family, one to his family, and two to friends. Just those four contacts resulted in hundreds of people being called. I was frantically put on prayer chains around the country.

If the Lord had plans to take me or have me suffer some of the horrendous side effects, with all those prayers going out, He must have changed His mind. Twenty-four hours later, every test came back negative. My vision was not impaired. My kidneys and liver were fine. I was alive and unharmed. As my recovery became more secure, I became the hospital joke—especially when they ran out of alcohol. Nurses ran around asking if anyone had alcohol hidden in their lockers that they could pour into my IV. And I can't tell you how many "alcohol drip" jokes I've heard since.

It's hard for me to think about what I went through emotionally, but it was a lesson for me. As a family, we'd had many hardships during the two years before my poisoning. I had actually prayed for God to take me. I think God wanted me to realize what I'd be leaving behind if He answered my prayer. I can't tell you how grateful I am for that lesson. Now I know I'm not ready to go. Not yet.

I'm not going to live happily ever after. No one does. But I'm living. And as long as God doesn't want me to leave just yet, I'm going to keep on living, and laughing, and crying, and loving. I'm going to hold my children and look at their faces and watch them grow for as long as I can. And I'm going to make sure the ones I love—particularly my husband, who faced *What if?* with such compassion and bravery—will know how much they mean to me. . .so I won't need five minutes ever again.

Gramma Jan
by Jan Coleman, Auburn, California

I hadn't expected Grace to be at the park that afternoon. I resentfully wondered why she'd had to come at all. Couldn't I be the only gramma this day? I'd waited five years to know this child.

Grace touched my arm softly. "I've thought about you so much these last few years." She had been constantly in my mind, too—the woman who is grandmother to my daughter's child.

I thought back to the morning when Amy announced her pregnancy. She was seventeen. Being a single mom myself, I had struggled solo through all her rebellious episodes. Until that day, I thought we were past the worst.

"I'm going to place the baby for adoption," she said. "Will you help me choose the parents?" she asked. My heart jumped. I felt relieved that she was choosing life and two loving parents for this child.

"God will bless you for this, Amy," I said, drawing her close.

We sat cross-legged on Amy's bedroom floor, reading the couples' profiles. I prayed for the Lord to give us discernment.

We each rated the couples and compared notes. "I can't believe we both picked Keith and Leslie for number one!" Amy said with delight. She had interviewed the top three but was instantly attached to Keith and Leslie. The papers were signed shortly thereafter.

Not until the ultrasound revealed that the baby budding inside Amy was a girl did it all finally hit me. I could suddenly envision a precious infant looking exactly like Amy with big, brown, curious eyes. *You'll be okay,* I told myself. *This kaleidoscope of emotions is normal.* Leslie then assured me, "We want you to be a part of this child's life." What role could I possibly have? Leslie's mother had waited sixty-three years to spoil her only grandchild. How much would she want me hanging around?

In Amy's eighth month, her boyfriend jilted her. She and the adoption agreement totally fell apart. "I can't do this," she said. "I'm keeping this baby. She's all I have."

I knew she was changing her mind out of desperation. She was so young, so tender, so bruised—not ready to be a mother. Stubbornly, she laid out her plan. Collect state aid for a while, live at home, and find some job training. Would I help her? she wanted to know.

I was so tempted. I had a good job. I could afford to help Amy and offer so much to the granddaughter I loved so much already.

I wrestled for days. I remembered all the times I had rescued Amy from her consequences, trying to shield her from her mistakes, trying to make up for the loss of her father. I remembered David's prayer in Psalm 86:11: "Lord. . .give me an undivided heart." I asked God, "What is right in Your eyes for this situation?"

God reminded me that faith is doing the right thing regardless of the circumstances, knowing He will turn it to good in the end.

The right thing.

I knew what that was, but would it turn Amy from me? Would I lose her, too?

"I love you, Amy," I told her. "This is your decision, and I'll support you in it, but you must find a way to support this child on your own."

She was so angry with me she didn't say a word to me until the day she went into labor. Then she asked me to be in the delivery room with her. After Nikki was born, I went right home, unable to sort out my feelings. I spent almost all night on my knees.

The phone rang early the next morning. "Something's wrong with her," Amy sobbed. "They're putting her in an incubator. Oh, Mom, I've been praying to God all night. I'm so confused. I love her so much."

Nikki rallied and the crisis ended, but it gave God time to work in Amy's heart. "I've prayed about this, Mom, and I'm calling Keith and Leslie right now. I know it's the right thing. It's God's best for her." Our tears were bittersweet.

Needing to say good-bye, Amy brought her daughter

home for one week. Those were special days to make memories with her first child: to hold her, sing to her, write her a loving letter, and then let her go. I couldn't get too close. I was afraid that embracing this child would only increase my sorrow when she left us.

When that day came, Amy could not stop weeping. We went straight to the Bible, to 1 Samuel. We talked about Samuel's birth being a testimony to the faith of a mother. "It wasn't easy for Hannah to give him up to be raised by someone else," I said. Yet Hannah was blessed with more children to take the place of the one for whom she prayed.

Just after Nikki's first birthday, Keith's job transferred him from California to Florida. Sure, I would get pictures and videos, but how would she ever know me at three thousand miles away? And as the years went by, the pain grew with every photo I received. Nikki was the image of my daughter. I felt so cheated. I was so angry with God.

When Nikki was five years old, the family made their first trip back to California. Could I meet them at the park? they asked. All the way down the freeway, I selfishly hoped Grace would not be there. I didn't want to compete for Nikki's attention. How would she respond to a woman she didn't know? "She knows she's adopted," Leslie had told me on the phone. "We're not sure how much she understands, but you are her Gramma Jan."

She was a delightful, loving child. We played hide-and-seek and fed the ducks. She sat on my lap and I fixed her ponytail while Grace sat quietly in the background. I was ashamed of my attitude.

At the end of the day, Grace took me aside. "You've done better than I thought you would, Jan. I know how hard this must be for you. She's a special child. She's such a blessing to me. Thank you," she said, squeezing my hand.

Tears stung my eyes. She was thanking me! Nikki was her gift from God, a gift that had come through me. I had missed Grace's joy because I focused on my loss instead of the good that had come from it. I had forgotten that God had ordained this adoption. He has a plan for Nikki's life, and He chose the part that I will play in it.

I glanced back at Nikki and said, "Thank you, Grace, for having room in your heart to let me be 'Gramma Jan.' "

The Day I Lost My Dad's Fishing Hat
by Jon Alessandro, Grapevine, Texas

Splash! The water was cold and murky. My dad's favorite fishing hat sailed off my head as I scrambled, trying to keep my head above the water. I knew I was about to drown, but all I could think about was my dad's fishing hat.

As a rule, my dad did not spend a lot of time with me as I grew up, but on rare moments, we braved life's storms together. Once, when I was about eight years old, we fished for trout at one of Dad's favorite fishing places with his buddy Ed. My dad let me wear his favorite fishing hat. The hat was really rather ugly. It was orange with brown splatters around the brim. My dad's last words to me that morning were, "Don't lose my hat!" I was proud and felt like a real fisherman. After all, the hat made the man. It didn't matter if you knew how to fish or not. If you had a fishing hat, you were a real fisherman.

We arrived at the fishing area early that Saturday morning and set up a small day camp. Ed prepared a hearty breakfast using a Coleman stove placed on the truck's tailgate. After breakfast, we gathered our gear. Each man went his own way, searching for the perfect fishing spot. I hopped a little stream and wandered into the valley, searching for a good place to settle in and fish. I poked around here and there and even tossed in a line now and again. No feeling is quite like enjoying the smell of fresh, clean air and the babble of a brook beside you. I wasn't having much luck fishing, so I decided to venture farther out. Before I knew it, I was bogged down in ankle-deep muck. I tried to wade gracefully through the mire, carrying my fishing pole and gear, but eventually I was covered in this awful-smelling gunk. I decided to head back since it was starting to get late.

I ended up on the opposite side of the creek from where I actually needed to be—beside a fast-moving section of the creek that was five or six feet wide. By this time, I was muddy and tired. The other side of the creek didn't look far away, so I decided to jump across it. I landed smack in the middle of the creek. At eight years old, I had little experience swimming, so I panicked, screaming and thrashing in the water.

Dad's favorite fishing hat was the first thing to go. I remember seeing it out of the corner of my eye, the brim filling with water as it was steadily taken downstream. All of my gear disappeared, too. I yelled, "Help! I can't swim!"

Ed heard me and called out, "Where are you?"

I went under and remember being quite amazed at how cold and deep this creek really was. I managed to break through to the surface and grabbed some weeds growing on the bank. I held on as the water swirled about me. I felt very heavy. "Help! I can't hold on!"

"Hold on! I'm coming!" Ed called back. I felt like I was going to sink back under the water. I gasped and choked and grabbed at more weeds, trying to find a better grip. The weeds began to give way. I heard the woods around me crash as Ed lumbered toward my location. The sound of his steps coming toward me comforted me.

"I can't find you; keep talking!" Ed screamed, panicking. I struggled at the creek bank and began slipping under the water. In a last desperate attempt, I pulled on the handful of weeds in my hands. My body surfaced a little, so I pulled at the weeds some more. Hand over hand, I began to pull myself out of the creek. As I rolled up onto the bank, I called out, "Never mind; I'm okay now."

I rested on the bank, cold, humiliated, and shaken. Then it dawned on me. My dad's favorite fishing hat was gone. I felt I should have drowned. I did not want to face my dad's anger. I got up and started to make my way toward Ed's voice. We finally ran into each other, and I could tell he was a little upset at not being able to find me.

Calmly Ed brought me back to camp, and we waited for the inevitable. Dad showed up a few minutes later, oblivious to what I had just been through. Ed didn't say anything as we packed the truck to head back home. As my dad climbed into the cab, I said, "Dad, I lost your hat."

Dad's face begin to turn all kinds of different shades. He started to lecture me on responsibility and trust. He made it clear that he was disappointed with me. He continued his diatribe as he put his hand on my shoulder, and then he stopped. He looked at me curiously and noticed how damp my clothes were.

"What happened?"

Ed broke in, explaining how I had fallen into the creek. My dad's face went from bright red to a sickening pallor. "You could have drowned!" He looked at me and said sheepishly, "I'm sorry, son."

Dad and I laugh about that day now. Every now and again, I'll ask Dad if he remembers the day I lost his favorite fishing hat. He sarcastically remarks, "Yes, and I still think you should have held on to it."

Sometimes I wonder if he means that, but I really know better. I know the love for a silly hat is worth far less than the love you have for your child. Jesus said in Matthew 6:26, " 'Look at the birds of the air; they do not sow or reap or store away in barns, and yet your heavenly Father feeds them. Are you not much more valuable than they?' "

My dad said he may have lost a hat that day, but he realized he could have lost something much more valuable: me. I think about this when one of my children stains the carpet with grape juice or loses a special toy. I can look at them and say, "I love you anyway. Did I ever tell you about the day I lost my dad's fishing hat?"

Bandaging and Bailing
by Alyse A. Lounsberry, Heathrow, Florida

Patti and I hit it off instantly. We shared a love of antiques, flowers, and interior design. She ran a small booth at a nearby antique mall where I worked part-time.

Patti was married to Clark, a Christian who had wanted to teach theology at the college level. Events and circumstances, however, had broken his spirit, robbing him of the necessary zeal to realize that dream.

Spiritually speaking, Patti was in worse shape than Clark. She had attended a Bible school, where a combination of misunderstandings and disappointments led to her being asked to leave the school—which she gladly did. She left the school, all right, but she left the faith, too. She walked away from God that day and never looked back, except in pain and anger.

That is, until the day we stared at the packing crates in the center of my living room, talking about my impending move to Dallas. Patti may have thought the move had come up quickly, but God and I knew the truth. I had prayed for more than a year for a this job in Dallas.

As we talked that afternoon, I knew I had to tread lightly

on the topic of faith. Every time I mentioned prayer and its role in my life, Patti bristled. So I would mention my prayers and then pull back. Then I would refer to my faith and pull back again. Patti began to rail angrily about how God had let her down and how mad she was at Him when the Holy Spirit whispered in my ear, *Tell her she may be mad at Me, but I was never mad at her!*

I sat there a moment, praying silently, until I was certain that He wanted me to speak those words.

In the middle of one of her tirades, I said, "God says to tell you that you may be mad at Him, but He was never mad at you!" Shocked, she just looked at me blankly. I could see the words bore straight through the concrete wall she had built around her wounded heart.

"Patti," I said, "I am moving away from here in a matter of days. I want you to know that we can pray right now, this minute. You can return to Him. He's not angry with you. He never was. Patti, I promise that until I move, I will pray with you and study with you and encourage you until you get your feet back on the ground with Him."

With tears spilling from her eyes, Patti prayed a simple prayer of repentance.

"God, I repent for judging You and for my anger toward You. I thank You that You loved me through the mess and that You were never mad at me. Thank You for receiving me back as Your child today. Amen."

We had lunch a few more times, read the Bible, and prayed. She asked lots of questions, which I tried to answer from my experience and study of the Word. Patti, it seemed, had become hungry again for the things of God. She was like a sponge, soaking up everything as if to make up for lost time. The woman I'd first met was now gone.

Her renewed faith acted as a tonic in Clark's life, too. They began to attend church, which became a place of healing and recovery, deliverance and discovery.

About a year and a half after my move to Dallas, the phone rang. I was delighted to hear Patti's voice on the other end.

"How are you?" I asked.

"Not so good," she confided. "I have just been diagnosed with stage-four lymphoma."

Stunned, I asked, "How many stages are there?"

"Four," she said.

"Oh, Patti! I am so sorry!"

"No," she said, "don't be. I'm calling to thank you for getting me ready for all this. I called to thank you for getting me ready for heaven."

As I sobbed, she thanked me. She revealed how much she had learned about God's love for her in the past months since she made that U-turn back to Him.

"I know He loves me and He's not punishing me with this," she told me. "But I also know I probably won't make it.

I'll fight like crazy to overcome this; but if I don't, I want you to know I'm ready to meet God because you cared enough to get in my face with some words I didn't want to hear!"

Patti didn't make it, but her bright spirit and courage in adversity inspired everyone around her. She touched many lives with the witness of her own life.

One of my own enduring images of Jesus is His "Samaritan" nature—His willingness to drop everything and get down into ditches alongside us, bandage us, and bail us out. He came for the broken ones among us, and those of us with shattered lives and dreams. When we need to recover, I envision Him bandaging and bailing so we can again walk in wholeness and love.

That's what He wants us to do for the "Pattis" among us. And that's what Patti did for others until the day she died. She told countless others how the Lord had taken her back even in her angry state, and how He'd take them back, too.

It's never too late for any of us to make one of these critical U-turns with God. He is merciful and full of grace. Call Him. He will answer you.

"What Was I Supposed to Be?"
by Lanita Bradley Boyd, Fort Thomas, Kentucky

I squinted in the glare of oncoming headlights. *Why am I keeping a seven-year-old up late on a school night?* I thought. Was the forty-five-mile drive to hear a Christian concert worth it? I was sleepy and questioning my parental judgment. I glanced at Kelsey. Eyes bright, she was obviously not as drowsy as I was.

"Mom, what was that song about with all the pictures of the doctor's stuff and teacher's stuff and children and old people and the baby's hand at the end?"

I had to think. Several of the concert's songs had been accompanied by slides. Then I remembered.

"Do you mean 'What Was I Supposed to Be?' " I asked.

"Yes, that's it. What did that mean?"

I took a deep breath. I was wide awake now, praying that my explanation would be complete and yet not frighten her. Hesitantly, I began.

"Honey, sometimes girls get pregnant when they aren't married." I could tell by her look I was already in trouble.

"But how can they do that? I thought getting married was how you had babies."

"Well," I groped, "sometimes teenagers do things before they are married—well, they act like—well, they do with each other's bodies what married people do. Then the girl gets pregnant. When she does, she has various choices."

I took a breath. "The girl and boy can get married if they love each other. A lot of people do that. Sometimes it works out to be a good marriage, and sometimes it doesn't.

"The girl and her parents can keep the baby and take care of it. Or the girl can give it up for adoption." I paused, considering my next words. "The way your birth mother did with you."

Kelsey brought me back to the point. "I still don't understand the song."

"The other choice is called abortion. That's when a doctor uses instruments inside the girl—a type of surgery—to get rid of the baby when it is still very tiny."

The voice beside me was also tiny. "Then what happens to the baby?"

"It's gone. The hospital gets rid of it, and the girl goes home. She isn't pregnant anymore." I hoped I was telling Kelsey what she could hear and comprehend.

"The song was written from the baby's viewpoint," I continued. "The baby was asking Jesus what it would have been if it had lived to be born."

I didn't know if any of this made sense to my little traveling companion until I heard her shuddering breath.

I glanced over to see tears streaming from her eyes. She caught her breath in short puffs.

Finally, she whispered, "Then that's what my birth mother could have done to me if she hadn't loved me so much?"

I eased the car to the side of the highway and stopped. I took Kelsey in my arms. We sobbed—and loved each other even more than before.

This gift of love from an unknown birth mother had changed my life forever. Tonight this song had made my little daughter aware for the first time of one of the greatest gifts of love—the gift of life.

Treasure Hunting
by Cheryl Norwood, Canton, Georgia

"Come on over tomorrow. All the children have gone through Granny's things, and now it's time for the grandkids to come and get what they want."

My uncle was in charge of disposing of my grandmother's things since she had lived with him the last few years of her life. Granny died from congestive heart failure but had been suffering from Alzheimer's for several years. In a way, we lost her months before her tired heart gave up and she went home to be with Jesus. Knowing she was no longer confused and scared but in the peaceful presence of God gave us comfort. Still, we missed her.

Granny had been a mother to seven, grandmother to more than twenty, and I can't even begin to count the great- and great-great-grandkids. My family is a diverse bunch. My cousins and I range in age from eighteen to forty-six. We represent just about every lifestyle—from rural country folk to urban yuppies. Managers and executives to blue-collar factory workers. Health-care professionals to secretaries.

Our only common denominator, the glue that kept us connected, was Granny. She loved the biggest rascal and scoundrel among us just as much as the one climbing the corporate ladder.

She made us all feel like we were the favorite! She could make us smile and talk and forget our differences and resentments. We'd do anything to see that twinkle in her eye and that face-splitting grin of hers. We counted on her unconditional love. When no one else cared, when no one else wanted us, we knew Granny did.

Granny never preached to us. And her love spoke volumes about God's unconditional love. In her own quiet way, Granny was our John the Baptist—pointing us to Christ. I suddenly wanted more than anything to find something of hers that would keep her in my heart.

Soon I was down in the basement apartment where she had lived, surrounded by boxes and tables piled with her belongings. I wandered from pile to pile, feeling compelled to touch everything, as if somehow I could connect with Granny through the platter she had piled high with biscuits; the pressure cooker she canned with; the blankets from her bed. Had I ever noticed that she liked little pig figurines? Was it being a seamstress that had given her such a love of scissors?

As I opened her closet door, I realized that this was where I got my love of bright colors. Red, purple, bright blue. There was the dress she wore to church the weekend she stayed with us. Here was the housedress she liked so much.

On one table were all her treasures, the gifts she had been given over the years. These included mementos and travel trinkets. Although Granny never wandered far from home, her children and grandchildren traveled all over the country—

some even internationally. Granny had traveled through us and had been with us in spirit wherever we went. Her prayers followed us everywhere, whether to college or to war.

I was amazed at how much compassion and understanding she'd had for so many of her children and grandchildren who had strayed so far from God's best for them. She loved her lost ones as much as Jesus did. I believe she would have done anything to see some of us not take the paths we had taken. I know she rejoiced when we turned back to God. Either way, she loved us. Even at the end, when she could not put a name to a face, she loved us.

One of my cousins visited Granny a few weeks before she passed and asked her, "Do you know who I am?"

"I can't say your name, but I know I love you," Granny replied.

This love made it so hard to decide what I wanted. There were so many precious items. I wanted to find things that reflected the intangible gifts Granny had given me.

I chose a glass oil lamp. Granny came from humble beginnings, and this lamp had not been bought for decoration. It served a purpose. Granny had lived many years without amenities yet had always been joyful. She was a light to her family; this lamp would help me shine God's light in the lives around me.

I took an old iron, the kind you heat up on the stove. Granny worked hard all her life, without many advantages and luxuries. Yet she did everything she could for her family.

She cooked, sewed, and worked. I thought about her hands grasped around the handle of that iron, and the prayers she said for her family as she pressed their clothes and linens. The iron would remind me to pray for others every day.

Next was a pearl-beaded purse with two rows of rhinestones. This purse reminded me that once upon a time, my grandmother had been young. She had gone to parties; she had danced. She had fallen in love and giggled and agonized over which dress to wear. This purse may have been the finest thing she ever owned. She kept it to remember to stay young at heart. I would keep it to remind myself that everyone I meet was once young and still has dreams. It also would remind me to keep dreaming!

Last, I took a little ceramic pitcher from Yellowstone Park. I don't know who gave it to her; I don't really care. It reminds me that all of us were her world. She lived through us and now she lives in us.

No matter where we go, no matter how far, she will always be there. She lives in my love of bright colors; she dances in my uncle's great sense of humor. Her spunk and spirit thrive in Aunt Alice. Uncle Danny and Uncle Alvin look at the world through her soft brown eyes. In each of us is a part of her. The same Jesus who lived in her heart lives in ours. One day we all will be together again. These little earthly treasures remind us of that most important promise, and for that I am forever thankful.

Warmed by God's Love
by Malinda Fillingim, Rome, Georgia

The summer season was long and hot under the South Carolina sun. I was serving as a missionary with migrant workers who were picking crops for two months. I worked with the children while their parents picked the crops. The compound where these hardworking folks lived was a fenced-in kennel type of dwelling. No privacy, little hygiene, and only a dirt road for the children's playground.

I tried my best to tell these sweet children about God's love, how Jesus had died for them, and how life was precious. But it seemed a hard message to sell amid their poverty, their seeming lack of hope for a bright future, and the overwhelming odds against their future including more than working in the fields. But I persevered. I learned their language, Spanish. I gave them clothing and food, and I helped the parents make a better summer for their children.

Puppet shows were a big hit. The parents enjoyed watching the shows just as much as the children did! I lost sight of the heat and poverty as we grew to understand one another and appreciate the fellowship we shared. But every evening I left the compound and returned to the air-conditioned, nicely furnished room where I lived. I had running water, a private bath, a nice bed, a car that ran well, all the food I wanted, and a future that did not include poverty or a nomadic lifestyle. I lived in two different worlds—one by day and one by night. I had an escape route. Did they?

As I contemplated my role in combating poverty, in helping to transform lives for God's glory, I began to wonder if I was making any difference. What good was teaching a few songs, a Bible story, a few educational sessions?

The week before the people were scheduled to move "up north," Maria came to me with a special request. She was worried that her children would get cold as they traveled north and lived in colder climates. Did I have a blanket to give her? One that was soft and could keep her three children warm at night as they cuddled together on the floor?

I searched local churches, but none had blankets during the summer. I didn't have enough money to buy one. So I reluctantly told Maria I had not found a blanket. She cast her eyes down and thanked me for looking.

As I lay in bed that night, I felt the soft quilt that covered me. How I loved this quilt. I had worked many extra hours to buy it a few months earlier. It was a beautiful blue and white quilt, with a simple pattern called "Wagon Wheel." It reminded me that life is a full circle, that we are all somehow connected to one another and to God. I felt safe under this quilt.

I began to wish I could get a quilt like this for Maria and her children.

When I woke up the next morning, I knew what I should do. I folded my prized quilt, placed it in a trash bag, and put it in my trunk.

Maria opened it with great glee. "You give this to me?" she asked with appreciation and curiosity.

"Yes, I do, with great love."

"Yes, I see the love."

I still think about that quilt. I have never been able to afford another one. But I know I am much richer because I allowed Maria to see my love, to know God's love, and to know how precious she is to God and me.

Quilts come and go, but God's love forever keeps us warm and safe.

One Small Loaf of Bread
by Kris Decker, Blaine, Minnesota

"Man does not live on bread alone" (Luke 4:4). I'd heard the verse all my life. But eleven years ago, I learned a person could live quite well on bread when it comes from a divine source.

I was only thirty years old, living in the rubble of my once carefully constructed life. My six-year marriage had crumbled, I was raising my daughter alone, and I was working two jobs to provide for us. Anxiety settled over me as my bank balance dwindled and my debts mounted. Just when I thought things couldn't get worse, my ex-husband stopped paying child support. No matter how many hours I worked, I couldn't earn enough to make ends meet without that monthly check.

Although I was on my own financially, I received emotional support from people I'd recently met in a support group, and from my neighbors, who were all Christians. They told me if I turned my life over to the care of my loving Father in heaven, He would help me. I had to admit it sounded good. But like those ads I'd seen posted on power-line poles—"Lose thirty pounds in thirty days"—it seemed too good to be true.

I moved forward cautiously. Instead of my spiritual journey

being a leap of faith, it was more like tiptoeing toward trust. Warily, I accepted my neighbor's invitation to church.

Much to my surprise, it was a pleasant experience. The people were kind, and the doctrine made sense. Everything should have clicked right into place, but it didn't. My heart was shut tight. I was afraid. What if I did turn my life over to God and declare Jesus as my Savior? Did He really care about what happened to me? And who was I to even ask for help anyway?

Then a small loaf of bread arrived.

"At long last, the famine has ended! Look what I got today," I announced to my friends, dropping the freshly baked bread onto the table. They all stared, confused by the roll of my eyes. "I got it from that church I've gone to a couple of times," I explained. "They give this to all the new attendees." I laughed scornfully. "If this is God's way of feeding us, we're going to starve within a week."

It was the worst kind of cruel joke. Only the day before, my mailbox had bulged with bills. The mortgage company, the electric company, and the city water co-op all tossed out threats like hand grenades: foreclosure, disconnection, discontinued service. I didn't know where I was going to get money for food. Our refrigerator and cupboards echoed from bareness, and I wouldn't get a paycheck for another ten days. That small loaf of bread seemed to mock my situation. I could lose everything, and if this was God, why was He sending me this one pathetic loaf of bread?

My friend Beth reached across the table and patted my hand. "Maybe this is God's way of letting you know He's going to take care of you," she said kindly.

"Yeah, right," I muttered. I had plenty of reasons to feel cynical about getting assistance from God.

It wasn't that I didn't believe in Him. If anything, I believed too well the lessons I'd learned as a child in our "religious" home—memorizing doctrine that taught me I had to earn the trip to heaven. All of my life I'd felt like a kid selling candy for a school fund-raiser, never quite producing enough good acts and ultimately falling short of my quota and the grand prize: an all-expense-paid trip to paradise. Even more discouraging was the belief that God didn't really know or care about me personally. He was just too busy with more important things, people had told me.

Well, if God doesn't care about me, I decided, *then I am certainly not going to care about Him.* And I locked the door to my heart.

Later that evening, after I'd taken my bread home and tucked my daughter into bed, I sat down to think. One of my friends had given me a Bible promise book that listed biblical promises related specifically to issues we face. I glanced through it.

I'll just see what God says about money, I thought. The defiant part of me wanted to challenge this seemingly foolish belief, while another part hoped to find some fiscal advice in those pages. Randomly I flipped open the book, not to "Money" as I'd intended but to "Faith." The verses all but jumped out of the book and shouted in my face.

" 'Believe in the Lord Jesus, and you will be saved— you and your household' " (Acts 16:31).

" 'I have come into the world as a light, so that no one who believes in me should stay in darkness' " (John 12:46).

"Then Jesus declared, 'I am the bread of life. He who comes to me will never go hungry, and he who believes in me will never be thirsty' " (John 6:35).

I know God's voice is often a still, small one—a whisper, a breeze, a gentle nudge. But that night was different. Like Saul of Tarsus, I needed to be blinded by a magnificent flash of light to see the truth. And I was, for there before me, spelled out in black and white, were the answers to every one of my problems—the house payment, the electric bill, the water bill, and food. If God had taken out a full-page ad in the *New York Times*, His message could not have been more obvious. The very thought of it took my breath away. At long last, the door to my heart flew open and completely off its hinges.

I sank to my knees, and for the first time in my life, I cried out to God for His help. For the first time in my life, I believed God heard.

Two days later, I received a phone call from the pastor

at the bread-giving church. He said he wanted to meet me. When he arrived at my home the following evening, I barely opened the door before he began to speak. He practically danced into my living room.

"I received a very clear message from the Holy Spirit concerning you," he said, smiling. "Here."

He pushed a paper into my hand. A bit frightened, I unfolded the paper. It was a check for $1,000—the amount I needed to pay all of my bills and buy food.

The pastor told me it wasn't a loan, and no strings were attached. I didn't need to do anything to deserve or earn this money. It was a gift, just like God's love. Just like Jesus' sacrifice on the cross.

I don't remember much else about that night. I think I was in shock, dazzled to think the creator of the universe did love me. How could someone so divine love me?

Even after all this time, I am still amazed by God's grace. God's intercession didn't end with the delivery of that check. Two months after I received it, I lost my house to foreclosure, my car to the junk pile, and my jobs to cutbacks and layoffs.

Like any good Father, God wanted not only to care for me but also to teach me. Once I truly believed I wasn't too insignificant for God to love, then I needed to build on my faith, lean on God instead of the world, and trust He would always take care of me, even in the worst of times.

And He did. After I lost my material possessions, I discovered my life didn't end. In fact, the more I lost, the richer I became. When I surrendered my life to God, He set me on a new path and blessed me. Within two years, I married a man rooted in his faith in God. God gave us a second beautiful child and provided me with miraculous opportunities to complete my education and begin a new career. He presented me with a quality of life, happiness, and peace that could come only from a benevolent Father who knew all along what was best for me—the kind of Father who could take a small loaf of bread and feed me with it for the rest of my life.

The Prairie Dwellers

by Lydia S. Ure, Windsor, Ontario, as told by Reverend Whiting

The beginning of my ministry coincided with one of the hardest times in American history. These were the toughest and best years of my life. In May 1929 I traveled west by train to my first pastorate. I was eighteen, dressed in my new gray suit, with most of my belongings in my dad's suitcase. I planned to evangelize everyone I met across the prairies. Some of my friends were being sent to city churches and would be paid well. But I would preach in farming communities and had no idea what my wages would be.

My elder met me at the station in a Model T. For the prairie dwellers, as the farmers were called, this would be a hard decade. From 1929 until 1939 no rain would fall, with the drought complicating problems of the Great Depression. We would not get out of this crisis until World War II (1939–1945) brought jobs.

Millions of acres of land became wasteland with thousands of people leaving behind everything they owned. When the drought hit, the earth turned dry and dust storms filled the air. Dust covered everything inside homes, and you could taste the grit in your mouth.

The drought affected twenty-seven states. The Dust Bowl area included parts of Colorado, Kansas, New Mexico, Texas, and Oklahoma. With no crops to sell, families went to bed hungry. Some nights I did, too, but people shared what they had. One woman in her seventies, dressed in a faded housedress, would bring ten cents' worth of sugar in a little brown bag and drop it into the collection plate. Another woman told me, "I have six in my family, and my share is two turnips. Here's half of one of my turnips." She wrapped this in newspaper and handed it to me. I cooked it for dinner that day.

Many times my parishioners invited me for dinner, but sometimes I refused because I knew they had so little and would go hungry.

One rancher, Clarence, walked six miles to attend a prayer service. When he learned I was taking on another school church, he said, "It will take some money, and they can't pay you. I was going to buy some boots when I sold my oats, but I'll give you the money."

A few days later, Clarence sold his oats. "Here," he said, handing me his money. "You do what God wants you to do. I can get other things for my boots."

I didn't want to take the money, but I knew a refusal would offend him. He wanted to do this to further the Lord's work. That Sunday as I preached, Clarence sat in his usual place up front. He had tacked pork rind on the worn soles of his boots. There he sat with flies zooming around his feet. But that was Clarence, a loving, faithful man of God.

In 1935 the federal government formed the Drought Relief Service and eventually provided $525 million for drought relief. The rains finally came in 1939 and ended the ten-year drought.

After fourteen years of ministry in the prairies, I left with my wife and two children for Pontiac, Michigan, with a greater understanding of faithfulness, sacrifice, compassion, and love. I had watched farms turn into wasteland but had seen souls filled with the Holy Spirit. The prairie dwellers, the prairies, are a part of me now. I will always remember those American moments as the best of times.

One Lost Sheep
by Elizabeth Griffin, Edmonds, Washington

When Curt Adams answered a call to join an outreach team in New York City, he had no idea that God was calling him to be His shepherd.

Early one morning, a week after the World Trade Center buildings collapsed, Curt and three other men from his church in Mount Vernon, Washington, climbed into a van and headed east. After forty-nine hours, they joined others in New Jersey and went to Union Square in New York City. Their mission was to minister Christ's comfort to the thousands at a twenty-four-hour candlelight memorial service.

With the stench of burning buildings stinging their nostrils, teams of Christians listened to, prayed for, and wiped away the tears of a mourning crowd. They came as Christ's body to support and heal.

As one woman shared the story of Nicodemus with another, Curt noticed a man listening. Just as Nicodemus had approached Jesus in secrecy, this man was edging closer. Curt then began to talk to the man. Omar, a Middle Eastern man who followed the religion of Islam, told Curt, "There are times that I want to know Jesus, and times that I don't."

Curt explained the gospel, emphasizing God's grace for each of us. When Curt said, "God wants you to leave your sin behind to follow Him," Omar quickly responded, "Yes, that's what I want!" They prayed, and one lost lamb was brought into the Lord's fold for all eternity.

The Lord had called a man to drive all the way from Washington State to New York City just to find one lost sheep. That's how much He loves us.

A Child's Explanation
by Michelle Guthrie Pearson, Leaf River, Illinois

I woke up at 6:45 a.m. when my son jumped into bed with me and we enjoyed the morning cartoons before getting up.

Around 8:30 a.m., horrifying scenes took over the TV screen. News anchors looked for words to describe the gruesome images. As I watched from the safety of my Midwestern farmhouse, the World Trade Center towers collapsed. My four-year-old son asked, "Why are you crying, Mommy?"

"Because sometimes bad people do bad things, Sean. And this was a bad thing." I hugged him. "Sean, I love you so much, and I'm so glad you're here with me."

I made the beds, cleaned the kitchen, and hung laundry to dry. The television played during my household tasks, bringing developments of the tragedy. My son played in his bedroom, uninterested in the drama.

That evening, we heard the president speak about the need to trust in God and the need for our nation to unite. I saw touching scenes such as London's Buckingham Palace Guard playing "The Star-Spangled Banner," and members of Congress singing "God Bless America" on the steps of the Capitol.

The following day, more hard news about the tragedy continued. Feeling the need to get away from the television, I loaded my son into the car. Already, things were changing. A car drove by with an American flag draped over the back windshield and over the trunk. The flags at the fire station flew at half-mast. A sign outside a doctor's office asked people to pray for peace.

"Mommy, if everything happens for a reason, why did God let planes crash into those buildings?"

"I'm not sure, Sean," I answered. I knew his question had no simple answer.

We took lunch to the park. My senses were heightened as I noticed everything around me. The scent of the prairie flowers, a butterfly landing on a cone flower, a brilliant blue dragonfly dancing with the summer breeze, the edges of autumn on the trees. These creations had always been there, but today I noticed them more than ever.

My son, whom I thought hadn't paid much attention to the news, ran to me from the playground.

"Mommy, do you think God always wins?" he said, his big blue eyes focused on mine.

"What?" I replied.

"Do you think God always wins? Maybe the devil won this time. Maybe that's why something very bad happened."

"I don't know, Sean. The Bible says there is a purpose for everything under heaven. I'm just not sure we can understand what that purpose is right now," I told him. He wanted answers, but I didn't have any.

"Well," my son said thoughtfully, "maybe the devil didn't win. Maybe the devil made this happen, and God knew about it. But maybe God knew it would make people love each other more. You know, be nicer to each other, like last night on TV. Maybe He knew it would make people sing."

Sean's explanation made me think of one of my favorite Bible verses, Ecclesiastes 4:12: "Though one may be overpowered, two can defend themselves. A cord of three strands is not quickly broken."

Sometimes it takes a child to remind us to make a U-turn and look to God for answers. Our faith and trust in Him will create a bond not easily broken by the enemy—in triumph or in tragedy.

Wisdom and Wrinkles
by Karen O'Connor, San Diego, California

"Karen, Cliff died the day after Christmas." My heart pounded at the sound of my friend Glenda's voice on my answering machine.

My husband and I had just returned from a glorious trip to Mexico, and this shocking news startled me back to reality. Cliff had died of heart failure, leaving his wife, their two children, and two teenagers from his previous marriage.

I couldn't get my mind off little Sarah, eight, and Brian, six. Their daddy was gone. Besides that, their maternal grandmother had died two months earlier, and their paternal grandparents had died two years before that. Their maternal grandfather was terminally ill, so he couldn't be present in their lives; and their only uncle and his family lived in Alaska—thousands of miles away. Sarah and Brian had experienced so much loss so early in their lives; I could hardly take it in.

The following Sunday, my husband and I invited Glenda and the children to brunch after church. While seated at the restaurant, Sarah seemed listless and disinterested in talking or eating. Brian picked at his food and clung to his mother as we talked.

Suddenly a thought came to me. I leaned over to Sarah and

asked if I could rub her back. "When we're sad," I said, "sometimes it helps to have someone who loves us touch us or hold us close."

She moved a little but didn't say anything, so I gently massaged her back and stroked her long hair. Within moments, she sat up and snuggled close to me. My eyes filled with tears.

"Since you don't have a living grandma," I said, "I'm wondering if you'd like to adopt me! I have gray hair and wrinkles and ten grandchildren, so I qualify, don't you think? And I sure do love you."

That did it. Sarah nodded her head yes, then drew closer. A moment later she straightened up and smiled. "Would you like to stop by our house and see the goldfish my dad gave me for Christmas?" she asked.

"I'd be happy to," I said. "I'm glad you asked."

We went back to the house, looked at the fish, and played a game. Then as I moved toward the door after saying good-bye, she called after me with joy in her voice: "Bye, Grandma. I love you!"

While walking home, I thought, *Lord, what have I done? I'm afraid I acted out of compassion in the moment, but I don't know if I can keep this commitment. We already have so many grandkids of our own.*

Then ever so gently, I sensed the Holy Spirit impressing on me that God had assigned me this special job and that He would give me all the resources I needed to do it.

God has been faithful, continuing the good work He began. It has been four years since that incident, and I have never once felt a lack of love or lacked the necessary grace to keep my commitment as Grandma Karen.

Father's Love

written for Mildred Hussey by Ruth Hess, Xenia, Ohio

"You won't bring any crazy religion into this house!" my dad yelled at me from his rocking chair in the living room. He jumped up and shook a clenched fist in my face to emphasize his feelings toward any daughter of his taking the name of Christ.

Minutes later, I sat in my bedroom listening to my parents shout. I heard the door slam, and a sudden quiet descended over our home. My eyes welled with tears.

I had always longed for a father who would love me no matter what. Now at the age of fourteen, I finally understood there was just such a Father available to me. He just didn't live at this address.

From the day I was born in that warm little bedroom off the kitchen of our home, I had seemed a misfit. As if it were not enough that I was not a son, the difficulty of my birth resulted in what my father thought were mental and physical defects and caused him to reject me throughout my childhood. To understand that your father has no use for you makes it all but impossible for you to flourish.

One afternoon two years earlier than my father's outburst,

two smiling people had arrived at our front door. They offered a free bus ride to church the next Sunday. Since my father, who did not always live with us, was away, Mother gladly accepted the invitation. I could hardly wait!

The church wasn't the attraction for me, but the bus was. In London in 1932, buses were just becoming widely used. We were overjoyed to be treated in such grand fashion. I was twelve years old and just beginning to understand my limitations and feelings of inadequacy because I wasn't "right in the head," as my father so often told me.

I was immediately awed at the sight of the huge Victorian mansion that had been transformed into what would become the center of my life. The people at Central Baptist Church loved and accepted me just as I was. They didn't seem to think I was crazy at all. The nervous condition that I'd been hospitalized with twice during my early childhood faded like a bad memory as these people began to love me to Jesus.

It took two years for the wounds to heal, but my heart began to break as I understood the love of Christ and my hope of a future in heaven. One Sunday, as tears fell, I bowed my knees to Jesus. With this one decision, I knew a brighter future lay before me. But I had not counted on my father's anger.

The door slam that day ended a bitter chapter of my life. Christ began to write His story on the pages of my heart. My father walked out of our lives, and I began to understand that despite what my father said, I had been perfectly created by a

God who loved me and had a wonderful purpose for my life. My heavenly Father began to build the confidence and assurance I would need in order to walk with Him.

God was faithful. The dear people of my church encouraged me through the early teen years when I quit school and got a job to help support our family. When God provided a wonderful young man from that church to be my husband, no one was more surprised than I was. When He called us into the ministry after World War II, I still could not believe it.

Last summer I visited the church of my youth. I found my seat in the balcony where Christ had spoken to me so many years ago. With tears, I made the same pilgrimage to the front of the church. Kneeling in precisely the right place, I gave thanks to God for taking this little nobody, giving her a Father who sent His Son to die for her, and transforming her into His servant.

A life full of opportunity and joy passed before my eyes as I remembered my wedding vows I shared at that very spot. I recalled the joy of my husband's ordination to the ministry in that same place and the thrill of walking through those doors as a young mother carrying the first two of my four children to proudly enroll them in the nursery.

When I left Central Baptist Church that day, I felt renewed gratitude that God gives hope. He holds Himself out to those of us who are hurting from all sorts of hopeless situations, and He calls us to Himself, where we find refuge and strength and love.

Children Are a Gift
by Maryella Vause, Blanco, Texas

In mid-December, a Texas Blue Norther swept into the hill country west of Austin. Temperatures dropped twenty degrees in twenty minutes. My husband and I drove over the frozen, rutted back roads across cattle guards to a small farmhouse just as an icy rain began to fall. *Swell,* I thought, *just what we need now.* My hands and my heart were cold. I was mad at God and mad at my husband.

We were on our way to attend a birth that I considered to be far less than a blessing. Didn't God's Word say children are a blessing, a heritage, a gift? How could He let this happen? *Why would You send a child into a situation like this?* I ranted in my heart. *People who would bring a child into an environment like this surely don't deserve a baby.*

The first time we were asked to attend a home birth, I thought my husband would just say no. I was shocked when he said, "We'll pray about it." We had never considered delivering babies at home. With our training, we knew the risks, not to mention the possible legal tangles and the scorn of our peers. But our local hospital had closed, leaving many of our patients with either untrained granny midwives or expensive obstetrical care at distant hospitals.

That first home delivery was the child of a regular patient. The birth was a beautiful, deeply meaningful, blessed experience for each of us. It was a joy to welcome the baby into a loving family. However, it also established us as the doctor and nurse who would deliver babies at home—exactly what I dreaded and feared. On the other hand, I admired my husband's willingness to help when no one else would. Maybe his experience as a medical commander in Vietnam during the Tet Offensive had given him the courage to think of others instead of the risks to himself.

When he had answered the phone this particular night, I knew he was tired. As the only physician in our part of the county, he worked sixty to eighty hours a week. I thought he would say, "Call EMS and have them take her to the city." My heart sank as I heard him say, "We'll be right over."

"Don't go," I pleaded. "You said that we would do these home births only at the Lord's direction. Surely He's not directing this. Did you even pray about it?"

"Yes, I prayed about it," he answered irritably. "That poor old woman is trying to deliver the girl by herself. God wants me to go. You don't have to come."

Right. How could I not go with him?

The girl lay in the drafty bedroom of the dilapidated old farmhouse. Hardly more than a child, she writhed in pain with each contraction. The macho boyfriend swaggered around in the front room while I helped begin coaching her to focus on her breathing instead of her pain.

The boyfriend was a local boy who had dropped out of high school to take up truck driving as a cover for drug running. He had brought this pathetic seventeen-year-old girl back from California on one of his "runs." When she was well along in her pregnancy, he dumped her at his mother's shack. His mother had called us, begging for help. Wearing a cowboy hat and boots, and grinning from under a two-day stubble of beard, the boyfriend extended his hand to my husband. "Hey, Doc. Glad you could make it. *My boy's* about to be born."

Oh no, I inwardly groaned, *one of those.* Could this possibly get worse? Just then the girl screamed, and he went three shades of pale. So much for his bravado.

"I'm going into town now to tell my buddies." As he reached for his faded blue jacket, my husband put his hand on the young man's shoulder and said, "You can't leave now. You've got to help us get the baby here."

With a look of fear, he said, "No way, Doc. I can't do that. I'm going down to the café, and you can just call me when the baby gets here. No offense meant, but having babies is women's work. I'll set off some firecrackers when my son gets born." He started to back toward the door. My husband caught his arm.

"You don't understand, son. We need you to help. We don't have a hospital here. Without those nice delivery tables, *you've* got to hold up her shoulders and be our birthing bed. You're strong. You can do it."

As I set up the bed and the room to receive the child, my husband showed the truck-driving cowboy how to support the mother's head and shoulders during the birth. I was annoyed. How could God send a child into this mess? The poverty, an out-of-wedlock birth, the risks to the mother, the risks to us. . .it all seemed so unfair to the baby.

We encouraged the mother as she became focused on delivering her child. We worked together, sweated, and prayed. Within two hours, the baby girl slipped into my husband's strong, gentle hands. When he placed the wet little one on her mother's breast, I looked at the young father. He was tired from holding up his girlfriend's shoulders. I was surprised to see tears running down his cheeks. He was gently stroking her hair with one hand as the fingertips of his other hand caressed the newborn's head. As he continued to stare, enthralled, at his daughter, he whispered, "Ain't it a miracle, Doc?"

I looked at the three of them: mother, father, and child. Suddenly I saw a family! Maybe not a "perfect" one, but, I thought, what right had I to judge? After settling mother and child and leaving instructions, we packed up to leave. Holding his baby girl, the young man thanked us repeatedly. As we left, he said, "Hey, I still gotta go out and shoot off some firecrackers. My buddies gotta hear that *my girl* is born!"

Our ride home was quiet. We were too tired to talk. I wondered what the future would hold for those three. I felt it was such a shabby, rough start. I prayed it would get better for them.

Well, he did run out and shoot off firecrackers. More important, though, he quit drug running and went into legitimate trucking. St. Ferdinand's Catholic Church beside the Blanco River never saw a sweeter couple take their vows. They stepped into a new chapter of their lives. Heavenly light shone through the stained-glass windows of the chancel as the ancient, yet timely, words were exchanged.

As husband and wife, they set up housekeeping in their own little home. They have had two more children. He has become a stable, upstanding member of the community. He waves and grins as his truck meets our car along the highway these days. She smiles and chats with me when we meet in the grocery, often telling me how well the children are doing in school. Sometimes she shows me the latest pictures of them, or I notice one of the children's names on the honor roll in the local newspaper.

When I see this family in the town today, I remember that cold, stormy night so long ago and ponder the fact that "His ways are not our ways." It still amazes me that God would entrust the care of a baby to us. He even placed His only Son as a helpless infant into the hands of a teenage girl. I still blanch when I remember my judgmental stance that night. I never would have sent a child into such circumstances.

God in His wisdom and mercy did!

"Behold, children are a gift of the Lord."

My Daughter's March to the Sea
by Diane Gross, Warner Robins, Georgia

I have never been so swept off my feet as when my youngest daughter sent me an essay she had written for her college English class. Each time I read it, I cry. I want to share this story with others.

"A MARCH DOWN TO THE SEA,"
an essay by Andrea Gross

"You sit on the suitcase while I try to zip it up," I said as I stuffed an extra pair of socks in at the last second. My little brother, overjoyed at the chance to be destructive, took a running start and jumped on top of my suitcase with an energetic, "Geronimo!"

This was to be a trip to remember, or at least, I was determined that it would be. Spring break of your senior year in high school happens only once, and I had one chance to make a memory that would last forever. Although I was going with my family to visit my sister in Saint Augustine, Florida, I was sure I could conjure up some unsupervised fun in the sun.

Early the next morning, I wearily opened one eye as the door of my room creaked open. My father, clad in an aroma of Old Spice, tiptoed up to my bed, which had not yet been visited by the light of day. With one fell swoop, he lifted me into his big arms and carried me to the ready-made bed in the van so my brother and I could snooze away the wee hours of the morning. I was always secretly awake during this part, though I never let my father know it. There was just something about being sixteen and still getting carried to the car by your dad. As long as he thought I was sleeping, I was glad to still be Daddy's little girl.

My family had always been close. We even went to church together every Sunday. Soon, however, our trip to the beach would change my life in a way I had never imagined.

On our second day at my sister Donna's house, she suggested that we do a Bible study together. This was not unusual for my family, so we gathered around the coffee table as she read from 1 Corinthians.

The words she spoke pierced my heart. Although it was not the first time I'd read the passage, this was the first time I listened to what it said. She read, "Do not be deceived. Neither fornicators, nor idolaters, nor adulterers, nor homosexuals, nor sodomites, nor thieves, nor covetous, nor drunkards, nor revilers, nor extortioners will inherit the kingdom of God" (1 Corinthians 6:9–10 NKJV). My face suddenly felt hot. I swallowed hard in a vain attempt to smooth the lump in my throat.

A thought crossed my mind so loudly that I thought others might have heard it saying, *If that's true, then I have no hope.* I certainly had not been living my life by that standard, even though I called myself a Christian and went to church every Sunday. The next thing I knew, my eyes were filling with tears. I pretended to sneeze so I could wipe them away. Then, in the middle of my hopeless despair, she continued to read the next line (verse 11), saying: "And such were some of you. But you were washed, but you were sanctified, but you were justified in the name of the Lord Jesus and by the Spirit of our God." Those words were like a breath of fresh air to my condemned heart.

I knew I had to change. I had been living the life of a hypocrite, saying I knew God and yet I knew I did not. Church had been one thing to me, and my private life had been something else.

I decided, then and there, to beg for God's forgiveness and the strength to return home to a new life, for indeed, I felt like a new person. I finally understood the verse that says, "Therefore, if anyone is in Christ, he is a new creation; the old has gone, the new has come!" (2 Corinthians 5:17).

That day, on the beach at Saint Augustine, I marched down to the sea with my sins strapped on my back, and I unloaded them into the water. I held my breath and submerged myself in it. When I came up, I breathed freely for the first time in my life, having been baptized by God Himself in His mighty ocean. The spring break of my senior year blew my expectations out of the water. I had hoped it would be a memorable experience, and as I have now learned, God never leaves you disappointed.

—THE END—

My daughter's essay was her testimony, and it moved me beyond belief. When Andrea walked toward the ocean that afternoon so many years ago, neither Donna nor I understood what was going on. All three of us had been reading when Andrea had simply and quietly stood up and walked into the water until she was completely under. It scared me so badly I stood up, wondering whether to run to her or not. At the moment I stood in fear, she blasted joyfully out of the water, hands held high in the air. Then she just walked back out of the water, returning to our blanket with the giddy grin on her face of a child who knew a secret. I told her often that she was a different girl after that day on the beach. I didn't realize until I read her essay that God had reached down into the sea and assured my daughter of His forgiveness and love, and none of us have been the same since!

Tea and Crackers
by Gail Hayes, Durham, North Carolina

These days I see God's love in the smallest things. One morning while watching a praise and worship video tape, I marveled as my two-year-old daughter blew on her toy clarinet, moving with the music. I felt she was caught up in the wind of His power. It was simply beautiful. The Lord immersed me in the flood of His love with my baby. Looking at this scene, it was hard to believe that not so long before this, the thought of having a child made me cringe.

As the firstborn girl of seven, the last thing I wanted was a child. I helped my mother with my siblings, and during my young adulthood, I just wanted complete freedom. I wanted freedom to do what I wanted, when I wanted, and how I wanted. Then suddenly my freedom collided with the brick wall of my actions' consequences. At age twenty-two, I was unmarried and pregnant.

I did not know the Lord and decided to terminate the pregnancy. I wanted that parasite out of my body. Yes, I called the life growing within me a parasite. I hated myself, so how could I feel anything for this child?

I entered the abortion clinic, wanting a quick and easy solution to my problem. The counselor was happy to explain that this was not a human life but merely a glob of tissue that needed to be cleaned out of my body. This would be a simple procedure, she said.

She took my money, covered my fear with smiles, and undressed me with deceit. I submitted myself and "this glob" to the abortionist's hand. Afterward I was served tea and crackers. I ate, not realizing the high price I would later pay for that snack.

I felt great relief as I exited the clinic, vowing never to go through its doors again. In a few months, I moved away from the Washington, D.C., area, hoping to start a new life, not realizing the devastating blow I had dealt to my body and spirit.

I had moved back home to live with my parents and attend school when I soon discovered I was pregnant again. Once again I had made a wrong turn, and once again I went to an abortionist. As a result of this visit, I attempted suicide and felt a deep self-loathing I would be unable to shake for years. This was payment for my second helping of tea and crackers.

Years later, after receiving the Lord, I discovered that I was grieving for those lost children. I turned to the Lord, and He did something miraculous for me. I fell on my face before Him and asked Him to open my womb. After eleven years of being barren, within two months of that prayer, I discovered I was pregnant. In my forties, He restored my lost children to me. Tears of unspeakable joy fill my eyes when tiny arms encircle my neck. With each hug, fragments of yesterday's torment vanish. With each kiss, healing balm fills my once-broken heart.

This is the depth of His love. He restored everything taken by the darkness of my past. He shined His light on the hidden treasures buried in my soul and gave me a future and a hope. He enveloped me in the sea of His love and washed me in the wave of His awesome forgiveness. My cup overflows with promises for my future. He anointed me with oil, draped me in royal robes, and placed a crown upon my head. I am His daughter, a daughter of the King.

His Word says He removes our sin far from us. Because of His mercy, I stand unashamed of my past. Because of His loving-kindness, I pray for those caught in abortion's deadly trap. I pray that like me, they will one day stand in the flow of God's love and not consume another snack of tea and crackers. Today I stand waiting to wipe fear's crumbs from hurting mouths and to dry lips dripping with guilt's tea. I stand waiting to love someone into the kingdom.

Reunion

by Gerry Di Gesu, West Chatham, Massachusetts

When one of my adopted sons, Chris, met his biological mother for the first time at the age of twenty-two, it was one of the most joyful days of my life. For reasons I don't fully understand, the idea of adoption still carries a mystique and a negative connotation for many people. That's why I want to share my joy.

When I told close friends that my son's birth mother wanted to meet him, I was surprised to find they assumed I would feel threatened and afraid. Actually, I was delighted.

I cannot imagine being either the mother of a child given up for adoption who never knows what is happening to her child, or being the adopted child who goes through life not knowing his or her background.

My husband and I had told Chris and his older brother, Kevin, that we would help them find their natural parents, but they had to realize it could be either wonderful or traumatic, depending on the person they found.

The fact that this woman had waited until he was twenty-two to inquire about him so she wouldn't disrupt his family gave me good feelings about her. Chris's easy acceptance of her invitation and his attitude convinced me he was sound and ready to cope with whatever he might find.

After interviews with the social worker at the agency that had made the placement, Chris and his birth mother met at the agency office. When Chris returned home from his visit, he had to rush to work, but he asked if she could come to our home later that evening. Of course we said yes; I was eager to meet her.

Later I opened my front door to greet a woman whose sparkling eyes reflected the joy of her day. We hugged and cried and then sat down to get acquainted.

Calmly she shared her story, relating the callous treatment she had received from her family, the social agency, and the hospital staff—none ready to offer compassion. She explained how desperately she had wanted to keep her baby and how only at the last minute, when she realized she couldn't care for him, had she signed the adoption papers.

She had been terrified of contacting the agency to find Chris, expecting harsh treatment, only to be delightfully surprised to find warmth and empathy instead. She battled the fear that neither my son nor his family would want to meet her. How I admired her courage to risk rejection each step of the way on her search for her child.

At last we finally said good night. I felt happy knowing I had a new friend and that Chris knew who he was and how much he was wanted. Time will tell how this relationship will develop, but I know that the look on my son's face and the joy in this woman's eyes as they said good-bye and hugged reinforced my belief that we can't be afraid—we have to risk and reach out in love. Christ did no less for us.

Project Founder

About the God Allows U-Turns Project Founder

Allison Gappa Bottke lives in southern Minnesota on a twenty-five-acre hobby farm with her entrepreneur husband, Kevin. She is a relatively "new" Christian, coming to the fold in 1989 as a result of a dramatic life "U-turn." The driving force behind the God Allows U-Turns Project, she has a growing passion to share with others the healing and hope offered by the Lord Jesus Christ. Allison has a wonderful ability to inspire and encourage audiences with her down-to-earth speaking style as she relates her personal testimony of how God orchestrated a dramatic U-turn in her life. Lovingly dubbed "The U-Turns Poster Girl," you can find out more about Allison by visiting www.godallowsuturns.com.

About the Contributors

Jon Alessandro is a freelance writer who writes frequently on Christianity and Christian living.

Pat Toornman Bales lives in Brighton, Colorado, on the farm she writes about in her story. Pat teaches school and writes books and short stories in her free time.

Tracy Bohannon of Riverview, Florida, is a mother, and has been a foster mother to a bunch of beautiful children.

Lanita Bradley Boyd is a mother, grandmother, writer, volunteer, and former teacher living in Fort Thomas, Kentucky, with her husband, Steve. She enjoys walking, reading, traveling, church ministries, working with Steve, and being with her family.

Candace Carteen has been writing since age eight. She is married to her best friend. They have one adopted son and are currently praying for a daughter to adopt.

Joan Clayton has written six books and more than four hundred articles. She is the religion columnist for her local newspaper. She and her husband, Emmitt, live in Portales, New Mexico. Her passion is writing. His is ranching.

Jan Coleman, from Auburn, California, is a busy author and speaker. She encourages hurting women to trust in God's promise from Joel 2:25 that God will restore the years the locust has eaten.

Kris Decker lives with her husband, Dennis, and children, Caitlin and Ryan, in Blaine, Minnesota. She is a freelance writer, artist, and editor of *Esther*, an E-magazine for women who long to be the person God wants them to be.

Gerry Di Gesu lives on Cape Cod in Massachusetts. She says, "If we look hard enough even on the darkest days, there is always a ray of hope somewhere—life is good."

Alex and Dawn Edwards live in Chicago with their son, Julius, who is the light of their lives. Dawn is a full-time mom and a freelance writer. Alex is an insurance executive.

Susan Farr Fahncke of Kaysville, Utah, is a freelance writer and runs her own Web site. She has stories published in numerous books and magazines.

Malinda Fillingim of Roanoke Rapids, North Carolina, is an ordained Baptist minister. She finds great joy in being the mother of Hope and Hannah and the wife of David.

Elizabeth Griffin lives in Edmonds, Washington, and is a wife and the mother of two young boys. She enjoys writing in her spare time.

Diane Gross lives in Warren Robins, Georgia, and is a mother of four, grandmother of four, and a published author and poet.

Gail Hayes is an international speaker and writer. She had her first child at age forty-one and her second at age forty-three. She lives in Durham, North Carolina, with her husband, R. Douglas, and their two miracles, Joshua Matthew and Gabrielle Christina. E-mail Gail at gmhayes@daughtersoftheking.org. Visit her Web site at http://www.daughtersoftheking.org.

Mildred Hussey was rescued from an uncertain future at the mercy of an unloving father when she came to fully rely on a new relationship with her heavenly Father. Her daughter, Ruth Hess, retells this story as an encouragement to others that their life, too, can change when they understand the heart of their heavenly Father.

Sara Jordan lives in Limestone, Maine. She has been a magazine writer and editor, as well as a writer of short stories for several anthologies.

Alyse A. Lounsberry, who lives in Florida, is a former senior editor with Word Publishing and section editor for the *New York Times* newspaper chain. She writes to encourage and inspire Christian women.

Carrie Mikolajczyk-Russell is a mother of two children and is married to Steve. She is also a surrogate mother to three children, and a business owner dedicated to helping infertile couples.

Cheryl Norwood lives in Canton, Georgia, just north of Atlanta, with her husband, Mike, in a small World War II bungalow. She has been published in several anthologies.

Karen O'Connor is an award-winning author and popular speaker for church and professional events.

Michelle Guthrie Pearson lives in Leaf River, Illinois. She is a free-lance writer whose personal relationship with Christ began when she met her husband, Jeff. They and their children live on a fourth-generation family farm in northern Illinois.

Harry Randles lives in Hot Springs Village, Arizona. Born in upstate New York in 1919, he "flew the Hump" in World War II. Since earning a Ph.D., his career has been in education: public schools, Syracuse University, and Vanderbilt. Now retired, he spends his time reading and writing.

Lydia S. Ure is a pastor's wife in a Windsor, Ontario, church plant. She was a volunteer at the local hospital for many years but now devotes her time to her husband, children, grandchildren, and freelance writing.

Maryella Vause lives in Blanco, Texas. She is a wife, parent, teacher, nurse, writer, volunteer, and Web master. She taught preschool through university, was a school nurse, then a family nurse practitioner for over twenty years. She is the mother of five and grandmother of seven.

John P. Walker lives in New Cumberland, Pennsylvania. He worked as a radio announcer before answering God's call to ministry. He pastors the West Shore Brethren in Christ Church near Harrisburg, Pennsylvania. John lives with his wife, Bonnie, and daughters, Charity and Stephanie. His passions include writing, photography, and skydiving.

Jill Lauritzen Zimanek, a native of North Huntington, Pennsylvania, lived in Iowa, Tennessee, and Wisconsin before moving to Athens, Georgia, with her sports editor husband, Brad, and two children. She is also a mom and a Sunday school teacher.

If you enjoyed

Journeys of Love,

check out the other books in this series. . .

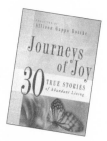